CERAMIC SKILLBOOKS

Series Editor:
Murray Fieldhouse

Clays

Frank and Janet Hamer

PITMAN/WATSON GUPTILL

PITMAN PUBLISHING LIMITED
39 Parker Street, London WC2B 5PB

Associated Companies
Copp Clark Ltd, Toronto · Pitman Publishing Co. SA (Pty) Ltd,
Johannesburg · Pitman Publishing New Zealand Ltd, Wellington
Pitman Publishing Pty Ltd, Melbourne

First Published in Great Britain 1977

Published simultaneously in the USA by Watson-Guptill
Publications, a division of Billboard Publications Inc.,
One Astor Plaza, New York, NY 10036

© Pitman Publishing 1977

Library of Congress Catalog Card Number 77—199

UK ISBN 0 273 01085 9 cased edition
UK ISBN 0 273 01000 X paperback edition
US ISBN 8230—0589—5

Text set in 10/11 pt IBM Century, printed by photolithography,
and bound in Great Britain at The Pitman Press, Bath

Contents

Introduction

Clay users are heterogeneous, from those who prospect from the ground up to those who buy convenience clays, wheel-ready or mould-ready, from those who work alone to those who constitute manpower, from those who seek artistic expression to those seeking economic viability. Nevertheless, their practical needs are surprisingly similar.

Clay is that marvellous creative substance upon which pottery, ceramic sculpture and architectural ceramics are based. Our lives are enriched by the direct expression held in these forms. We also depend upon clay for tableware, sanitary ware, electrical insulators, bricks, cosmetics and in paper and rubber.

Sometimes dry, powdery, shaley or sticky, sometimes smooth and fine or coarse-grained, in colours of blue, grey, white, yellow, pink, buff or terracotta, clay is common to most parts of the world.

Chemically it is composed of the commonest of elements: silicon, oxygen, aluminium and hydrogen; but it has two important and unique characteristics. Clay can be given a form which it retains, and it can be changed by heat from a mutable to a durable material.

This book describes the origin of clay, its chemical and physical make-up and its properties of workability and drying. It explains how to retain and improve these properties by knowledgeable preparation, how to make up clays for specific purposes and gain from their special characteristics, and gives advice on purchasing clays.

We are indebted to researchers and clay suppliers, especially R. W. Ford, W. Ryan, F. Singer, S. S. Singer, W. E. Worrall, English China Clays & Co. Ltd, Watts Blake Bearne & Co. Ltd. We acknowledge the assistance from others mentioned in the text and are grateful to Pitman Publishing Ltd for use of material

from *The Potter's Dictionary of Materials and Techniques* by
F. Hamer. The photographs and drawings are by the authors
except where otherwise credited.

We dedicate this book to all aspiring, inspired, determined and
successful potters.

Ponthir April 1976   Frank Hamer
                                                      Janet Hamer

1 The Origin and Geology of Clay

Rock into clay

All clays originate as deep-seated igneous or metamorphic rocks. Hot magma pushes upwards but does not reach the surface and therefore cools slowly in large masses. These are domes of rock created where the magma is prevented from making further upward movement. Such domes are the granite bosses which today form upland areas like Dartmoor in south-west England. While cooling and still in thermoplastic state, the future clays are subjected to infiltration by hot gases pushing their way upwards. These gases include boron, fluorine, carbon dioxide and water which in two stages of substitution decompose a potentially hard rock and create a soft one which includes clay. The clay content is unlikely to exceed twenty-five per cent of the overall bulk of rock involved.

Granite engenders a pure clay which is referred to as the mineral kaolinite. Its crystal structure is ordered (strictly regular) and strong. Natural clays as they are dug, are less than perfect, but the crystals of china clay approximate to the mineral kaolinite and are accorded this quality.

The less pure clays originate from rocks other than granite. Such rocks are both igneous and metamorphic, that is, both the hot molten rock pushing upwards from the earth's interior and the country rock which is changed by heat and pressure through its proximity to the igneous intrusion.

The parent rocks of the less pure clays look similar to granite but are darker in colour. Their difference is one of chemical composition. They contain many more chemical elements and their structures also are more complex. This is why they engender the less pure clay which in mineral terminology is called disordered kaolinite. The name refers to the crystal structure which is distorted in comparison with the strictly regular kaolinite one.

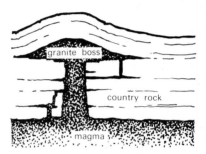

Fig 1. The creation of a granite boss where the hot magma is limited in upward movement.

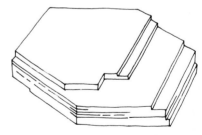

Fig 2. Clay crystal magnified 150,000 times.

3

Kaolinite and disordered kaolinite are both clays but it is possible during decomposition for other mineral structures to be created which resemble clay, yet are not clay. Mica and montmorillonite are two. They are both group names. The micas are present in most clays when dug and are rarely described individually. Instead they are referred to collectively as mica or micaceous sand. They give a fine texture to the clay.

Montmorillonites are of exceedingly fine particle size and although present in clays in only small amounts they account for noticeable strength and plasticity. The natural material bentonite is nearly pure montmorillonite and is used to plasticize clay bodies. It so strongly resembles clay that it is often referred to as a clay although it is not of kaolinite structure. Beds of bentonite are found separately from clays as a product of the decomposition of volcanic ash.

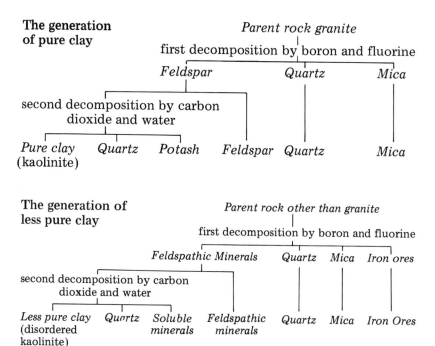

The generation of pure clay

Parent rock granite

first decomposition by boron and fluorine

Feldspar   Quartz   Mica

second decomposition by carbon dioxide and water

Pure clay (kaolinite)   Quartz   Potash   Feldspar   Quartz   Mica

The generation of less pure clay

Parent rock other than granite

first decomposition by boron and fluorine

Feldspathic Minerals   Quartz   Mica   Iron ores

second decomposition by carbon dioxide and water

Less pure clay (disordered kaolinite)   Quartz   Soluble minerals   Feldspathic minerals   Quartz   Mica   Iron Ores

Primary clay

Clays which are found in their place of origin are called primary or residual clays. The china clay of south-west England is a primary clay and it is possible that a few of the most refractory fireclays are primary also, but it is no longer possible to identify the parent rock. Bentonite is primary montmorillonite.

Secondary clay

Clays which are transported from their place of origin and settled elsewhere are called secondary or sedimentary clays. All the highly plastic clays like ball clay and red marl are secondary, and so also are some low plasticity clays like fireclays and the china clays of south-eastern U.S.A. (called kaolins in the U.S.A.).

There are a few wind-blown secondary clays but most secondary clays are transported by water and ice. Rain enters the cracks of the decomposed parent rock and in freezing, expands to loosen a section. Little by little over thousands of years the bulk of rock disintegrates, collapses and is washed away in streams and rivers, is eroded by sea or lake, or is scraped away by glaciers.

During transportation by water, the clay is subjected to impact and the already tiny particles become smaller still. Some associated minerals like quartz sand and mica may be separated from the clay by the process of natural levigation. A fast-flowing river can carry large and small particles, even large pebbles, but as the river reaches flatter ground it slows down and loses the energy necessary to move the heavier objects. The finest particles, and these are the clay ones, are carried the furthest before being deposited in a lake or on the sea bed. Even here there is a sorting of size. A clay stratum has a progressive variation from coarse to fine with possible change of colour and composition. Sedimentary clays rarely show a uniformity over a wide area, which is why blending of different clays is necessary to maintain a constant product.

When clays are transported by glaciers they are subjected to physical grinding. This produces superfine clays which are plastic and sticky. They accumulate where the glacier melts and thus are not levigated like water-borne material but are mixed with sand, gravel and rock. They are called boulder clays, which is an apt name

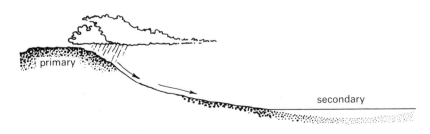

primary

secondary

Fig 3. Natural levigation from primary to secondary clay.

since the boulders often considerably outweight the clay content.

High and low plasticity clays

Plasticity and strength are important to potters using traditional forming methods. They are properties which make clay different from chemically similar materials, and they enable the potter to make an infinite variety of shapes with speed and confidence. Clays which lack sufficient plasticity for the job in hand are called short or lean clays. Clays which have abundant plasticity are called long or fat clays.

Plasticity is directly related to particle size. The finest clays are the most plastic and since through transportation the clay is impacted, ground, and finally sorted by particle weight, it follows that secondary clays are superfine clays. This gives the general rule that secondary clays are highly plastic while primary clays are of low plasticity.

The rule is usually applicable but it is too neat to be universal so there are important exceptions. Some secondary clays resist the acquisition of plasticity even though transported considerable distances with ideal refining conditions. Clearly the reason for this must lie with the clay itself — we have already seen that there are two types of clay structured as kaolinite and disordered kaolinite and born of different parent rocks.

The purest clay mineral referred to as kaolinite comes from the feldspar in granite. It has a laminar structure of alternate gibbsite and silica layers which is well ordered and thus strong. The result is a relatively large crystal, and when many crystals aggregate they tend to do so in an orderly way, producing a clay particle which is virtually one large crystal. This large crystal resists weathering and therefore the purest clays are never highly plastic. China clays and fireclays are examples of this, whether from primary site or secondary deposit.

On occasions, nature fortuitously creates superfine kaolinites giving freak clays in isolated pockets. Such plastic china clay enabled the Chinese to produce their superb thrown porcelain. Similar pockets are reported in the U.S.A. and Australia.

When rocks other than granite decompose, the resulting clay crystal cannot be the regular kaolinite. Some of the sites in the crystal structure are occupied by substitute atoms which disorder the crystal. Disordered kaolinite crystals aggregate in very random fashion to form clay particles and thus, even if pressured into shales, they have little compact strength. Such particles are readily broken down to extreme fineness. Even the crystal itself succumbs to weathering.

Disordered kaolinite clays are therefore the more plastic and their plasticity is a direct result of the substitute atoms within the crystal. These substitutes also give a dark colour and act as fluxes during firing. Some soluble minerals are washed away during transportation but others are attracted to the crystals. Secondary clays can be expected to contain a number of minerals extra to the clay mineral, and these are known collectively as 'impurities'.

Thus three very general rules of thumb emerge about clays: (i) that primary clays are low-plasticity clays while secondary clays are high-plasticity clays; (ii) that the lighter the colour of the clay, the more refractory it is, while the darker the clay, the more likelihood there is of its being a fusible clay; and (iii) that primary clays are more refractory than secondary clays.

Prospecting

Prospecting has romantic associations. For the potter it involves understanding something about geology, thus being aware of the likely places for clay deposits and looking with an enquiring eye. Large companies have already thoroughly investigated most countries for remunerative deposits so there is little likelihood of the individual discovering a miracle clay in large supply. But prospecting is based upon hope and in more than one case has resulted in a reasonable short-term supply. Many potters prospect only for small amounts which can be used as coloured slips and in glazes.

Prospecting is not confined to open country but is applicable everywhere. One rural potter realised that the best clay in the area was probably some five miles away in the valley and under the town centre. His opportunity to get the clay came with major alterations to the town centre when the excavations for foundations produced over a year's supply of excellent clay.

But for most potters a large supply is more likely to be discovered at existing quarries. Many brick quarries contain a seam of better clay which is mixed with the poor quality for brick-making. Quarry owners know their clays and generally are keen to discuss them with like minds. Hand-picking the raw lumps provides the best opportunity. Sometimes dust from the grinding pans and shredded or milled clay can be bought.

The Ordnance Survey geological maps are the obvious starting points for prospecting in the U.K. 'Drift' rather than 'Solid' maps are required because these show what is at the surface including the alluvial and glacial deposits, both of which could contain clay.

Fig 4. Opencast ball clay mine
showing stratification and digging
in progress. (*Photo supplied by
Watts Blake Bearne & Co. Ltd.*)

Rocks are divided into those of igneous origin like granite and
basalt, and those of sedimentary origin like limestone, coal and
clay. Generally speaking, the mountainous areas are composed of
igneous rocks while the lower land is sedimentary. For the most
part prospecting will be in the sedimentary areas while remember-
ing that the igneous areas contain small pockets of sediment often
of glacial origin.

While geology maps are extremely accurate, their information
is restricted to the evidence available at the time of the survey.
Small local deviations therefore occur in areas which could not
be surveyed in detail. There is always the chance of a lucky find.

It may be small but two thousand pots can be made from a cubic metre of clay! The prospector should investigate stream and river banks and new cuttings for pipe-laying, roadworks and building foundations. In this way a detailed knowledge is built up. Of course, digging must only be pursued with permission. The upper twenty to fifty centimetres of most stable land is weathered to soil and is called the overburden. This is why it is necessary to look where sections are exposed. Even so there are tell-tale signs like pools of standing water after heavy rain.

Clay provides a waterproof layer. Rain runs off hills composed of clay and shale, cutting deep channels in the surface, washing

Fig 5. House foundations expose the underlying stratum and possible locations of clay.

Fig 6. Clay banks erode into rounded spurs with deep fissures. Shrinkage cracks are noticeable in dry weather.

away and resettling elsewhere. Follow the streams and find where the clay has collected. Hills composed of porous rock and rocks with fissures allow the rain water to seep to the interior. The water eventually emerges at springs which can be located by a change of vegetation and are usually along a contour where the porous rock rests upon clay. Springs are marked on some maps. Look also for local names like 'clay hill', 'clay pit', 'brown hill' and interesting prospects like 'old levels' or 'disused quarry'. Thirty years of weathering in a disused quarry might have produced some excellent clay.

First tests

On-the-spot tests can tell us quite a lot about clay samples. Pinching a small pot is useful, as is doing a simple deformation test and a tie-a-knot test. In deformation testing, a piece of clay is pushed with the thumb or finger and we note how much initial resistance there is. Also we note whether the clay went in the way intended and whether it held the intended form. Some poor clays have too much initial resistance and feel hard and bouncy. Some have no resistance and stick to the fingers, spoiling the intended form. Others tear instead of sliding in the shear.

In the tie-a-knot test, a piece of clay is rolled between the palms to give a strip about the thickness of a pencil. This strip is tied in a knot. A good clay will accept this exercise without rupture. The poor clay will rupture if it does not actually break. These tests tell us about the clay's workability.

A rough idea of the throwing texture can be obtained from the bite and the palm tests. In the bite test, a fine section of the clay pressed between finger and thumb is gently bitten with the front teeth. What appears to be a fine clay reveals its sandy content in this way. In the palm test a dry piece of the clay is rubbed vigorously in the palm with the other hand. The fine clay is dispersed and the grit content remains. The feel of this action tells us

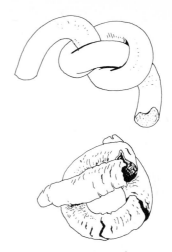

Fig 7. Plastic and short clays are assessed quickly by the tie-a-knot test.

Fig 8. The palm test gives an indication of the sharpness of the grit content.

whether it is a sharp or a rounded content. It may be quartz sand, feldspar or mica. A comparatively large grain is tolerable in throwing if it is rounded. Sand, feldspar and mica affect the glaze fit and thermal properties of the finished product. These minerals can often be separately identified by the use of a magnifying glass.

A clay's composition is also indicated by its colour: yellow, brown, green and grey clays contain iron. Clays in chalk and lime-stone districts are likely to contain calcium carbonate. Remember the general rules about clays. The light-coloured clays are the more refractory. For high-temperature work over 1250°C (2282°F) it is necessary to use these, but we cannot expect them to be as plastic as the dark-coloured clays. The darkest clays will fire to a range of progressively darker browns from 900° to 1100°C (1652° to 2012°F). Above this temperature they quickly distort and break down. Clays containing calcium carbonate even if light in colour will have a ceiling temperature of 1100°C (2012°F). The cream-coloured clays, the grey clays and buff clays are middle range clays useful in the 1150° to 1250°C range (2102° to 2282°F). Note the exception to the general rule: blue and black ball clays appear very dark but their colour is not that of iron; it comes from a high carbon content which burns away. Many ball clays are at their strongest when fired to around 1200°C (2192°F) and are blended with the more refractory clays to produce stoneware bodies.

A lot can be estimated about the probable firing properties of local clays but do not overlook the evidence which can be seen in the bricks transported from brickyards and in the bricks of old buildings in disused quarries, since these bricks are likely to be of the local material.

12

2 The Chemistry and Structure of Clay

Physics and chemistry are man's attempt to understand and classify nature. They are of help to the potter who is trying to assess the potential of a particular clay. Will it withstand stoneware temperatures? Is it sufficiently plastic for throwing? We rely upon our own experience of previous clays that we have handled, but we can also use the experience of others through scientific analyses when we understand something of the chemistry and structure of clay.

The chemistry of clay

We saw in the first chapter how granite decomposes into feldspar, quartz and mica, and then how some of this feldspar further decomposes into clay, quartz and potash. The second stage can be represented in chemical symbols as:

$$K_2O.Al_2O_3.6SiO_2 + 2H_2O \rightarrow Al_2O_3.2SiO_2.2H_2O + 4SiO_2 + K_2O$$

feldspar water clay (kaolinite) quartz potash

It is possible to use chemical symbols because the substances involved are all minerals and a mineral is a chemical compound, that is, two or more chemical elements combined in a predictable proportion.

In the equation clay is represented by $Al_2O_3.2SiO_2.2H_2O$. This is the pure clay mineral kaolinite. The symbols tell us that clay is a complex chemical compound involving three compounds in the proportion of one molecule of alumina (Al_2O_3), two molecules of silica (SiO_2) and two molecules of water (H_2O). This is a potter's approach. A chemist or a mineralogist would combine the symbols thus: $Al_2Si_2O_5(OH)_4$ and by this imply that the clay crystal is an integrated structure involving aluminium (Al), silicon (Si), oxygen (O) and hydroxyl groups (OH). The chemist is quite correct, as is shown by the study of the structure later, but the potter wishing to understand his clay cannot visualize these constituents whereas he has probably met alumina as a bat wash, silica as flint or quartz sand and water as rain. As far as possible we will retain pottery parlance for these chemical descriptions.

A second equation explains the firing of clay:

$$Al_2O_3.2SiO_2.2H_2O \text{ firing } Al_2O_3.2SiO_2 + 2H_2O \uparrow$$
$$\text{clay} \longrightarrow \text{pot} \quad \text{water vapour}$$

At the left of the equation is clay which includes two molecules of water locked up within the structure of the clay crystal. This is known as the water of crystallization or the bound water, although it is not present as water in the normal sense but as hydroxyl groups (OH). To drive out this water requires at least red heat. The process starts around $450°C$ ($842°F$), intensifies up to $600°C$ ($1112°F$) then decreases before $700°C$ ($1292°F$). Thus after the firing we have a completely new material which is different in physical properties, it is now hard and water resistant, and it is probably changed in colour also. The potter calls it pot, the chemist calls it dehydrated aluminium silicate and the mineralogist calls it metakaolin. The change from clay to pot is called the ceramic change. It is a once only process. It cannot be reversed.

Analyses

Analyses arose from the need to classify clays scientifically in order to define similarities and differences which are not made apparent by the simple tests described in the previous chapter. A pottery manufacturer expects his clay supplier to repeat last year's batch of excellent clay. The supplier must constantly analyse his raw material and either offer different batches or blend clays from different seams in order to keep within the defined analysis limits of his product.

Later in this chapter physical analyses are discussed which describe the mineral content and physical properties of a clay. But here we are concerned with the chemical content which is given by two types of chemical analyses: ultimate and fired.

Ultimate analysis
The ultimate analysis is the most useful to the potter. It is expressed as percentages of those metal and non-metal oxides that are involved in ceramic fusions. Elements and oxides which do

not enter the fusion are classed together as volatiles and labelled
'H_2O etc' or 'loss on ignition'. The oxides listed do not necessarily
exist in that form. For example the calcia (CaO) probably exists
as calcium carbonate ($CaCO_3$) in the clay. This ultimately becomes calcia in the firing and so for the ultimate analysis it is
described as CaO and loss. There is no significance in the order
of the list but there is an accepted practice which is used here for
ease of reference. The examples given are typical rather than
specific and serve as standards for comparison.

	china clay	ball clay	siliceous stoneware	red earthenware
SiO_2	48·0	55·5	66·0	60·0
TiO_2	0·1	1·5	1·5	1·0
Al_2O_3	38·0	29·0	20·5	20·0
Fe_2O_3	0·3	1·2	1·0	8·0
MgO	0·1	0·3	0·3	0·8
CaO	0·2	0·5	0·5	0·6
Na_2O	0·2	1·0	0·2	0·1
K_2O	0·3	3·0	2·0	2·0
Loss	12·8	8·0	8·0	7·5

When given an ultimate analysis of a clay we can compare
it with these four examples and should first note that the loss can
vary between four and fifteen per cent but this figure gives no
indication of what the loss is or whether it requires special consideration during firing. Also we should realize that a large
percentage of loss has the effect of making the other items appear
smaller than their true value when fired.

The simplest and most sure prediction is the colour from the
iron oxide (Fe_2O_3) content. Amounts up to one per cent will
hardly show. Between one and two per cent gives an ivory to
cream colour in oxidation and a pale grey in reduction. Between
two and ten per cent gives pinks to rich deep browns.

The alumina (Al_2O_3) content is an indication of refractoriness.
The range is from twenty to forty per cent which approximates a
firing range from 1050° to 1350°C (1922° to 2462°F) but this
cannot be taken as the sole guide to the fusibility or refractoriness of a clay. We must link this observation with that of the
fluxes.

The fluxes are magnesia (MgO), calcia (CaO), soda (Na_2O) and
potash (K_2O). A refractory clay like the china clay example
has a total flux content of less than one per cent. Vitrifying clays
have amounts up to five per cent and fusible clays up to ten per
cent. Soda and potash are responsible for a progressive vitrification over the whole range of firing starting around 800°C

(1472° F). Magnesia and calcia give a more vigorous fluxing from 1100°C (2012° F) which results in rapid vitrification and fusion. Clays intended for use over 1200°C (2192° F) should contain less than one per cent of combined magnesia and calcia. Assessment of fluxing action should be balanced with assessment of the anti-fluxing action or refractoriness of the alumina content.

Lastly the silica (SiO_2) can be considered and will be found to vary enormously, in fact between about forty and eighty per cent with variations of as much as fifteen per cent between clays which in use are surprisingly similar. Under forty-eight per cent is low and indicates a refractory clay if the alumina content is over twenty-eight per cent. Around sixty per cent silica is to be expected in vitrifiable clays. Over sixty per cent indicates a siliceous clay which may or may not be fusible depending upon the alumina and fluxing contents as previously discussed.

Fired analysis
In the fired analysis the content list is often simplified by grouping and the volatiles are discounted. A fired analysis is investigated in the same way as the ultimate analysis. Typical examples are given for comparison.

	china clay	*ball clay*	*stoneware clay*	*fireclay*	*delft marl*
SiO_2	53	57	63	55·5	64
Al_2O_3	44	37	32	41	15
Fe_2O_3	1	2	2·2	2·3	4
MgO + CaO	1	0·5	0·6	0·7	14
$Na_2O + K_2O$	1	3·5	2·2	0·5	3

Constituents of clay
The following are eleven common mineral constituents with descriptions of their contribution to the raw and fired properties of clay.

Kaolinite ($Al_2O_3.2SiO_2.2H_2O$) **and disordered kaolinite** are the clay minerals which provide the plasticity of the raw material and which change during firing to produce a permanent material.

Feldspars are many and variable. The commonest is potash feldspar ($K_2O.Al_2O_3.6SiO_2$). Feldspar can constitute twenty-five per cent of the 'clay'. It provides the progressive fluxing necessary for the mature vitrification of stoneware.

Mica ($K_2O.3Al_2O_3.6SiO_2.2H_2O$) is a close relative of and half-way between clay and feldspar. It is one of the minerals from the decomposed parent rock granite and provides useful fine texture in clays.

Quartz or free silica (SiO_2) is silica extra to that within the kaolinite, feldspar and other silicates. It is crystalline and exists as fine to coarse quartz sand. Impure sands are often coloured and give attractive speckling. Large amounts of free silica decrease plasticity, add refractoriness and extend the vitrification range.

Potash (K_2O) **and soda** (Na_2O) are present in feldspars and associated minerals. They are active fluxes over the whole range of pottery firing and responsible for the progressive vitrification of clays. Small amounts of free potash and soda affect the slippery property of clay.

Calcia (CaO) is often present in the carbonate form ($CaCO_3$) as a superfine chalk or limestone, and in combinations with ferrous carbonate. It also exists as partial substitutions in the feldspars and feldspathic minerals in clays. It bleaches the iron in clays producing beautiful yellow ochres, some of which can be preserved through firing though most turn to tan colours. In clays fired up to $1100°C$ ($2012°F$) calcia provides the valuable property of high contraction during cooling which inhibits the crazing of the overlying glaze. Natural clays used for this purpose are the malms or true marls which contain between five and fifteen per cent calcia. Above $1100°C$ calcia causes rapid vitrification because it is an active flux. Clays containing over five per cent calcia are often included in slip-glazes. Relatively large pieces of calcium carbonate and calcium sulphate occur in some clays and are difficult to remove except by fine sieving. They are insoluble lumps which, if not removed, decompose during firing to produce pockets of calcia within the clay. If the body is porous this calcia (which is quicklime) absorbs moisture from the air, expands and causes a flake of body to fall off.

Magnesia (MgO) is present in combination with calcia and attached to the clay crystal. It acts as a high temperature flux. It rarely exceeds three per cent of the clay.

Red iron oxide or ferric oxide (Fe_2O_3) is a red-brown soft crystal. Its particles are as small as clay's and therefore cannot be separated from the clay by sieving or levigation. The carbonate compound ($FeCO_3$) is common in clay shales. Iron also occurs within the clay crystal in partial replacement of aluminium. Iron oxide colours clay brown, and in combination with other minerals is responsible for clay colourings of yellow, grey and green which mostly achieve the buff to brown colour after firing. Iron sulphide or pyrite (FeS_2) occurs in fireclays. Very small particles give decorative speckles under reduction but large pieces cause unsightly eruptions.

17

Fig 9. China clay particles by electron micrograph showing the regular structuring of the kaolinite crystals. (*Photo supplied by English China Clays Co. Ltd.*)

Titanium dioxide (TiO_2) occurs in the structure of many silicates in partial replacement of silica. It combines readily with iron oxide producing and sustaining clean tan colours.

Water (H_2O) physically provides the necessary lubricant between the clay particles to give plasticity. It is also responsible for the character of this plasticity by its own chemical impurities. Although extremely weak these impurities provide either an acidic or an alkaline lubricant according to the electrostatic field of the adsorbed layers of the clay particles. The position of the clay particles in relation to one another (electrostatic attraction and repulsion) is affected by their relationship to the lubricant. Ultimately this positioning affects the fired ceramic. Therefore density/porosity and fired strength of the finished product depend to some degree upon the water in the clay.

The physics of clay

A single kaolinite crystal is of hexagonal shape about one-tenth as thick as it is wide. It is composed of hundreds of layers like the leaves of a book. In fact an average crystal enlarged 400,000 times would be the size of this book but hexagonal in shape. The

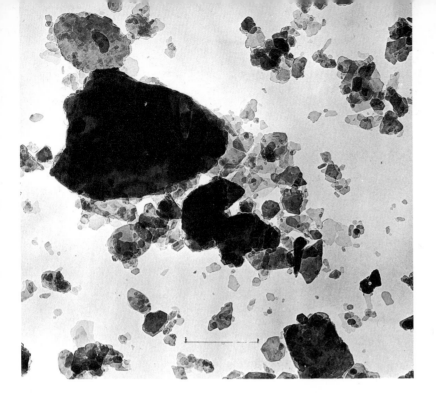

Fig 10. Ball clay particles by electron micrograph showing agglomeration of the disordered kaolinite crystals. (*Photo supplied by English China Clays Co. Ltd.*)

largest crystals to the same scale would be about a metre across, and the smallest ones less than a centimetre. These crystals must not be confused with clay dust or particles — they are so small that they are invisible to the naked eye, and many hundreds of crystals make up one particle.

The smallest clay particles are smaller than the wave-lengths of visible light and are also too small to be seen, but the largest particles are visible as clay dust or grains. Because of the electro-static forces of attraction and the compression that clays at rest have undergone, the largest grains are often replicas of the smaller crystals. That is, they are flattish and roughly hexagonal. The reason for this flat hexagonal shape becomes clear after studying the structure of the clay crystal.

The structure of the clay crystal

Oxygen is the most common element in the earth's crust, in the sea and in the atmosphere, and it is the linking force in clay. The clay crystal is composed of thousands of clay molecules arranged in strong sheets. A sheet is strong because it is composed of alternate layers of silica and gibbsite, both layers having oxygen

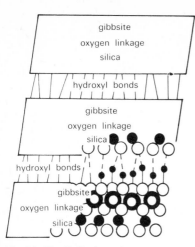

Fig 11. Kaolinite layering.

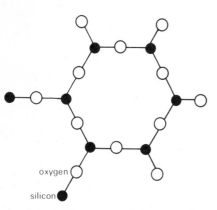

Fig 12. Silica layer of clay crystal structure.

as their major constituent forming the structures. Each silica layer is fastened to a gibbsite layer by oxygen links, and the combined silica-gibbsite layer is attached to others by hydroxyl bonds to form crystals. This is the kaolinite or clay crystal. The crystal approximates a hexagon when seen from above, and is strong in one direction but weak in the other. Figure 11 is a diagrammatic side view showing the silica and gibbsite layers linked by oxygen atoms and the composite layers held by hydroxyl bonds.

Since the structure is in sheets, it can be conveniently represented by a series of diagrams. As an indication of scale, six million of these diagrams side-by-side would equal one centimetre. Figure 12 shows the silica layer. Each oxygen atom requires links with two silicon atoms. The hexagonal structure allows this and promotes a sheet structure which can continue indefinitely on all sides but cannot extend from the oxygen atoms above or below. In this respect it is like the diagram which is flat on the page. However, each silicon atom requires links with four oxygen atoms and in this sheet there are links with only three. There is as yet insufficient oxygen to give the common silica formula of SiO_2.

Figure 13 shows how each silicon atom obtains its fourth oxygen atom. This is positioned above each silicon atom, thus forming a little three-sided pyramid out of the four oxygen atoms with the silicon atom fitting snugly inside.

The original layer shown in Figure 12 is now shown in dotted outline. There are now too many oxygen atoms to give the common formula SiO_2. This is because the top layer of oxygen atoms shown in figure 13 are as yet not attached to their requisite number of other atoms (their valencies are unsatisfied). The mineral form of silica known as quartz would result if the unsatisfied atoms of oxygen were to link up with more silicon and so on upwards. However this possibility is inhibited in clay by the presence of aluminium which forms the next layer called the gibbsite layer.

Figure 14 shows the strictly regular gibbsite layer. The presence of aluminium in six-fold coordination with oxygen (links with six oxygen atoms) makes a stiff and regular lattice. Part of this lattice is composed of the oxygen atoms from figure 13, here shown as dotted outlines. Their valencies are now satisfied by a link with silicon below and two weaker links to aluminium atoms above. The other oxygen atoms of this gibbsite layer have their unsatisfied valencies occupied by a hydrogen atom each. The total atoms in the composite sheet represented by figures 12, 13 and 14 are $Al_8Si_8O_{36}H_{16}$ which when rationalized gives $Al_2O_3.2SiO_2.2H_2O$.

The hydrogen atoms of the gibbsite layer do not form a rigid bond but are able to oscillate in their attachment between these oxygen atoms and other oxygen atoms in an adjacent layer. The adjacent layer is another composite sheet above of identical make-up. The hydrogen oscillation holds the two layers together by what is called the hydroxyl bond (Figure 11).

The theory of this structure will become clear if the three diagrams are traced on separate sheets of tracing paper. A different colour should be used for each element: oxygen, silicon and aluminium. One tracing is superimposed upon another to form the kaolinite sheet.

Substitution

Atoms of different but similar elements, e.g. iron, magnesium and aluminium, compete for sites within the structure of the clay crystal durings its formation. When iron and magnesium are present they will usually succeed in obtaining about one in ten of the sites into which they can fit. In the regular kaolinite these sites are all occupied by aluminium. The iron and magnesium atoms are larger than the aluminium ones and therefore distort the crystal causing points of weakness. This occupation of sites, which in the purest crystal structure are the homes of a particular element, is known as partial replacement or substitution.

There is also substitution within the silica layer. Aluminium sometimes occupies about one in fifty of the silicon sites. These substitutions have a two-fold effect. They weaken the crystal by distortion and they upset the overall electrostatic neutrality of the crystal.

Iron can occupy an aluminium site because it forms the same number of bonds with the surrounding oxygen atoms. It balances their negative charges with its positive charge and merely distorts the regularity of the gibbsite layer in order to fit in. But when magnesium replaces aluminium and when aluminium replaces silicon, the negative charges of the oxygen atoms are not complemented in full. These negative charges are balanced by the attachment of positively charged atoms like potassium, sodium, calcium and magnesium which are extra to the kaolinite structure and position themselves either inside the spaces which exist in the silica layer, or else attach themselves on the outside of the crystal. This addition of extra atoms to balance the overall electrostatic charge is called adsorption and the attached atoms are called adsorbed ions.

Thus it is seen how the chemical composition of the parent

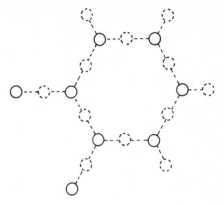

Fig 13. Oxygen linkage layer.

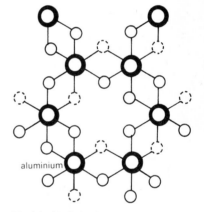

Fig 14. Gibbsite layer.

rock affects the type of clay to which it eventually gives birth. Granite contains little or no iron and magnesium, therefore the clay crystal cannot be distorted by them. Granite also contains over sixty-five per cent silica and consequently has abundant silicon atoms to occupy the possible sites within the clay crystal. On the other hand rocks other than granite contain iron and magnesium (mafic) minerals and are low in silica.

Physical analyses

There are three types of physical analysis which describe the mineral composition and physical make-up of a clay. They are the rational, proximate, and particle size analyses.

Rational analysis
The rational analysis is ascertained by actual isolation of the minerals concerned. The composition is expressed as proportions of pure clay (called clay substance), quartz, and either feldspar or mica. In the feldspar type the amount of clay substance is higher by fifteen to twenty-five per cent than in the mica type because a proportion of the mica is attributed to the clay substance, its nearest related mineral. Analyses by different methods give quite widely differing results so caution must be exercised in the comparison of analyses from different suppliers. Four examples are given.

	china clay	ball clay	red clay	fireclay
Clay substance	88	70	60	57
Quartz	9	27	31	31
Feldspar	3	3	9	12

A knowledge of the working properties of a clay is gained from these analyses when the amounts are linked with a particle size analysis. The amount of clay substance is an indication of how the clay will behave, plasticity-, strength- and shrinkage-wise. The quartz content is some indication of the textural 'bite' of the clay. The rational analysis is most useful in the comparison of a number of similar clays, as for example when a supplier offers ten ball clays.

Proximate analysis or calculated mineralogical composition
This analysis is calculated from a chemical analysis and re-expressed as proportions of kaolinite, feldspar (or mica) and quartz. The amounts are investigated in the same way as those of the rational analysis. However they are a less accurate indication of physical make-up than those of the rational type. Again those

from a single supplier are comparable and it should be noted that the assumptions they contain are made by people with a thorough knowledge of the clays concerned.

Particle size analysis
Clay particles are so small that they are measured in microns. A micron is one millionth part of a metre; to give some idea of the minuteness of this measurement, the holes in a 100's mesh are each 150 microns across! Particles of this size are measured by the speed at which they settle because the largest particles settle proportionately quicker than the finest of the same material.

Having collected the information, there are a number of ways of explaining it. One is to state what percentage of the material is less than a given size. This is useful if the size chosen is 1·0 micron in diameter because all this material is likely to be clay. Quartz and feldspar are rarely of sub-micron size. Take note whether the size given refers to diameter or radius. In the absence of 1·0 micron size, 2·0 micron is acceptable to denote useful plastic clay.

Better still is the analysis which lists a range of sizes as in the examples to follow. Occasionally the different constituent minerals are separately described which is even more revealing. The coarsest particles, or grains as they are called, are measured in mesh sizes and given as a mechanical analysis. This information is sometimes added to a particle size analysis by stating what percentage would be retained by a particular mesh. In the five typical examples the numbers state what percentage of the total matter is less than the particle size indicated at the head of the column. The sizes are spherical diameter equivalents in microns.

	0·5	1	2	5	10	20 *microns*	*retained by 200's mesh*
China Clay	18	30	42	60	75	90%	1%
Ball Clay	36	54	63	77	87	95%	1%
Stoneware Clay	17	43	59	72	79	83%	12%
Fireclay	12	21	32	46	58	68%	15%
Red Clay	22	33	47	67	76	82%	15%

It is immediately apparent that ball clay has a higher percentage of the finest particles than other clays, which is why it is so plastic. However, noting the one and two micron percentages, we see that the stoneware clay has a high clay content and so will be plastic and probably strong. In comparison fireclay has few of these one and two micron particles and will lack plasticity and strength. A potting clay requires at least thirty per cent of its

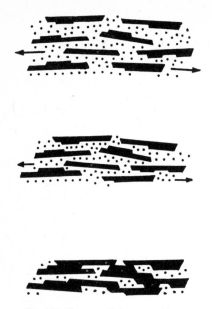

Fig 15. Clay particles are able to slide past one another when lubricated by sufficient water.

particles below one micron size. The 'coarse' material retained by 200's mesh gives some indication of quartz sand and/or clay shale content but it may not necessarily represent the clay as dug, but rather the clay as offered for sale.

Clay and water

Dry clay contains up to fourteen per cent bound water or water of crystallization (the two molecules of H_2O in the chemical formula). It is locked within the crystal and also exists as a chemically anchored layer of molecules around each crystal. This water is only removed by red heat during the ceramic change. But dry clay also contains pore water in the holes between the clay particles, and this water does not dry out because there is water in the atmosphere. However, it can be removed by heating the clay to just over $100°C$ ($212°F$), the boiling point of water.

Plastic clay contains additional water called water of plasticity. This accounts for between twenty and thirty per cent of the weight of plastic clay. This water dries out naturally in the air. Water of plasticity is the lubricant between the clay particles, and if there is plenty of water the particles can slide past one another without difficulty (Figure 15). A very soft, wet, plastic clay is in this state. When there is less water between the particles, there is some stickiness, like a wet pack of cards — a stiff plastic clay is in this state. As the water dries out of clay, the particles are brought closer together, and the clay object becomes a solid.

3 Workability

Workability is the standard by which the potter measures his clay in use. It is the character of a clay that is a combination of plasticity, strength and thixotropy.

A clay of good workability stands up well to the stress of stretching as in throwing, pressing, and the pulling of handles. This demands a combination of strength and plasticity. A good clay also has the capacity to allow itself to be shaped by a reasonably slight pressure. This is the property of plasticity which is first appreciated as an ability to 'slide' under pressure. Plasticity allows the solid to be reformed without rupturing and allows the new form achieved to remain without any attempt to return to the original form. That is, there is no elasticity involved. Covered by the term thixotropy is the capacity to provide the necessary strength and plasticity when needed. A clay for throwing and hand-building must reasonably support its own weight.

A clay which has these properties is called a plastic clay, or fat, or long clay, while one which lacks them is called a lean, or short clay. Short clays are difficult to knead. They have some capacity to slide, but they have a high resistance to pressure.

Many attempts have been made to measure plasticity. Their success has always been in a narrow field that required too many qualifying conditions. No overall measurement has been found that can apply to all potting circumstances. Yet every potter knows when he has a 'plastic' clay and when he has a 'short' clay. In estimating a natural or prepared clay's workability potential the true clay content is first assessed. Non-clay particles detract from plasticity since they exhibit little or no plasticity themselves. Common non-plastic constituents are pieces of shale, sands, quartz, mica and feldspar. The factors which contribute to the plasticity and strength of the clay content are all related to the size of the clay particles.

Plasticity and particle size

The smallest particle sizes give the most plasticity. The fineness of particle is not a question of a mesh size. The clay particles are infinitely smaller than could be separated by sieving. They are of near colloidal size and individually invisible to the naked eye. The largest size involved is in the region of three microns in diameter. Such a particle is that of a coarse clay which is not very plastic, e.g. china clay. In comparison, a ball clay has particles averaging 0·25 microns and bentonite 0·05 microns.

Plasticity and water content

Small particles present more surface area per given weight of clay than do large particles. Therefore there is a greater surface area to be surrounded by water in fine clays. Plasticity is obviously linked with moisture content. A stiff clay becomes more plastic with increasing amounts of water, but there is an optimum point after which increasing amounts give too much fluidity. Water can account for forty per cent of the weight of plastic clay. This forty per cent is made up of about twenty per cent lubricant, ten per cent to fill the pores between the particles of clay, and ten per cent chemically combined within the clay particles. The twenty per cent lubricant water, or water of plasticity, enables the particles to slide past one another. A fine ball clay can hold as much as thirty per cent lubricant water whereas a coarse fireclay may have only ten per cent. The more water a clay can hold without becoming too sticky to use, the more workable or plastic it will feel.

Strength and thixotropy

The strength of a clay is vital. Strength is derived partly from the structure created by clay particles and water, and partly from the friction between clay and non-clay particles.

The clay particles are flat hexagonal shapes. These plate-like shapes fit together in a brick-like overlapping structure, lubricated with water. Under pressure they will not break apart in a crack because of the strength of this structure. Instead they will slide sideways past one another. Uniformity of size and close packing increase this effect (Figure 16).

The flat faces of two adjacent particles provide an excellent suction area when lubricated with water, while the thin flat shapes also present a large surface area for very little weight. They therefore respond to the mutual forces of attraction or gravitational pull which, at the exceedingly small size of ball clay and bentonite

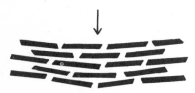

Fig 16. Bricklike structure resists direct pressure.

particles, become increasingly larger forces proportionately.
These forces of suction and attraction serve to hold the particles
together. They present a resistance to pressure, but when pressure
is applied to the clay there is a point at which this resistance is
overcome. This is called the yield point. Resistance to direct
pressure is high but once sideways movement is established, as
when a thumb is pushed across clay to test for plasticity, it
continues easily (Figure 17a and b). At this point the bonds between particles are temporarily broken as they slide across each
other. The shearing of bonds continues as a sequence of bonds
break and remake. On release of the pressure the bonds re-
establish themselves strongly to hold the new form.

This ability to remake bonds quickly and firmly is called
thixotropy. It is especially valuable when throwing on the wheel
where very soft clay is pushed and pulled quickly into a new
shape. Thixotropy enables the clay to stand in the new shape.

The presence of some non-clay particles by their less regular,
less flat shapes provides some abrasion which helps the clay wall
to stand up. They act as 'throughs' do in a stone wall. This is
particularly necessary for tall pots. The amount and size of this
matter is critical and must be correctly balanced with the plasticity and thixotropy of the clay (Figure 18).

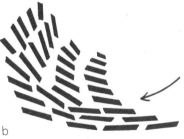

Fig 17. (a and b) Particles slide
under sideways pressure and then
hold their shape.

Fig 18. Grains of grog support fine clay in a newly thrown pot wall.

Fig 19. Overfine clay deforms under its own weight.

Fig 20. Too much coarse material allows the clay to rupture.

Clays with a correct balance of plasticity and friction will withstand the pull occasioned by their own weight in wide or tall free-standing clay structures. A clay with too much plasticity and insufficient friction collapses — it deforms by its own weight and uses its plasticity to enable it to do so (Figure 19). A clay with too little plasticity and too much friction also collapses, but it does so by tearing between the particles. Here the apparent strength is all in initial resistance to movement. Such clays are dead to knead and often have a stodgy or bouncy feel to them. They break under tension, and consequently cannot withstand that most crucial potter's test: the pulling of a handle (Figure 20).

The general strength of a clay is improved by bringing the particles closer together. The bonds and suction are increased even though the ability to slide, the plasticity, is not increased. Ageing, wedging, pugging, especially de-aired pugging, help in this way to improve overall workability and hence apparent plasticity.

Improving workability

Grain size
The first and sometimes only treatment needed by a newly dug clay may be the removal of surplus sand, shale or stones. The clay must be made into a thin slurry and run through the size of mesh which most efficiently removes the unwanted material. If the sand is too fine and sieving impractical, the process of levigation

can be used. This provides a very fine clay in the region of ninety per cent true clay content. It involves a very watery suspension and a lot of settling.

A clay will not exhibit its full plasticity potential if its fine particles have compacted into large grains. To break down these grains into particles it is necessary to soak the clay in water and age it or use a blunger, preferably of the high speed type. The more water that is available at any stage of clay preparation, the more plastic the final clay is likely to be because the water penetrates between and divides the particles giving more particles of smaller size.

Blending
If one has a clay that lacks plasticity, one can add this property by adding a clay of high plasticity. The resulting blend will be proportionate. Even ten per cent of a highly plastic ball clay will make a noticeable difference in the workability. It is sufficient to knead the two clays together in a plastic state, although it may also be necessary to add a little extra water. Ten per cent of a light-coloured ball clay will have little effect upon the colour of a clay; it will, however, affect the drying and firing shrinkages. Plastic clays have high wet to dry to fired shrinkage rates.

Plasticizers
Another way to improve plasticity is the addition of plasticizers. Plasticizers encourage the slipperiness of existing clay particles or introduce highly plastic particles to act as a lubricant for the clay and other materials.

Bentonite has very plastic particles (though strictly not a clay, it is so called). A clay which is very low in plasticity can be made workable by five or six per cent of bentonite. A usual amount added to many clays is one or two per cent. This is a dry weight measure of bentonite to the dry weight of the clay. However bentonite cannot be added as a powder to plastic clay. It must first be mixed with about twice its own weight of water so that it swells to a slippery mass rather like greasy soap. This is added to the clay by slicing the clay with a wire, poking holes in the slices and sandwiching the bentonite before rekneading. The bentonite provides so much 'slide' that the process is not an easy one. More than once through a pug-mill is necessary.

Other plasticizers which encourage slipperiness are polymerized carbohydrate pastes and bacterial colloidal gels.

The addition of plasticizers is an attempt to speedily produce a clay with the qualities it would naturally acquire by ageing and souring over many months or years. It is sufficiently successful to give the plasticity and thixotropy required for press-moulding and jigger and jolley forming where a high strength is not required, because the mould supports the clay. In fact a weaker clay is less likely to tear if well lubricated because it deforms readily. Such a 'doctored' clay may also be adequate for the quick throwing of simple shapes. The thixotropy however, seems to suddenly disappear when more prolonged work on the wheel for more difficult shapes is attempted. This is because the plasticity and thixotropy was that of relatively coarse particles. The flocculatory effect of the average sized clay particles had been encouraged to its maximum but the contribution of the very much finer colloidal particles to the strength of the structure had not been brought into operation (Figure 22a).

The full potential can only be realized by the developing process of ageing and souring.

A clay which is so highly plastic that it lacks workability is sticky and very soft. It deforms easily with little initial resistance, and lacks sufficient strength to support its own weight. This state of over-plasticity occasioned by a large proportion of extremely fine clay particles or by use of plasticizers can be mistaken for shortness by the inexperienced. The optimum correction for this state can only be decided upon after consideration of a few trials each involving additions of different materials. China clay, a sharp sand and a sharp fine grog can be tried. All these provide friction between the particles thereby adding strength.

Moisture content
The correct moisture content for a plastic clay is a matter of specialized choice. However, one could say that each clay has a moisture content amount at which its full plastic potential is realized. One should aim at knowing one's clay so well that this moisture content can be accurately achieved.

Slight alkalinity or acidity in the water of the clay can affect its plastic behaviour. For example, in the blending of two plastic clays from different sources, one is likely to find that one clay affects the other. The usual effect is that the slightly more acidic one opens up the other and creates space for more water. Two quite soft clays will then give a stiff blend which requires extra water to bring it to workable consistency.

One should also be aware of the effects of the acidic and alkaline waters in the clay, especially when throwing. Alkaline clays soften quickly. Alkaline water feels slippery but softens clay quickly. Acidic clays are often 'thirsty' to throw with, stand up well and then collapse suddenly. Acidic water can even be responsible for 'tugging'.

Ageing

Undoubtedly the best way to realize a clay's full potential for
plasticity, strength and thixotropy is by ageing. Ageing is used
as a synonym for souring although a difference can be inferred.
Clay can be aged in damp rooms, in airtight bins or by wrapping
in polythene sheets. It must be kept damp continuously or the
advantages will be lost. A warm atmosphere is acceptable if
humid, but frost should be avoided at this stage because it brings
the water out of the clay leaving it difficult to deal with by hand
methods of wedging and kneading. Weathering is an earlier stage
of clay conditioning which uses frost.

Fig 21. Water splits large grains when clay is ageing.

Ageing involves the slow penetration of water between clay
particles giving a net result of more particles of smaller size
(Figure 21). This means a higher plasticity. When the clay is put
to age, there should be extra water available in the clay. If this is
not done the clay cannot age properly and may be too stiff to use
after ageing. It is an easier process to de-water a clay slightly by
kneading on an absorbent surface than it is to add water and mix
this in.

Another action during ageing is the slow compression of the
clay particles. A stack of clay is compressed slightly under its own
weight. Particles which are closer together have more strength.
They are held together by suction with the seal of water. Providing there is water between the particles, the full plasticity will be
maintained. The compressed clay has increased workability.
Compression can be achieved without ageing by vigorous wedging.
A good pugmill will also compress the clay but the ideal simu-
lation is a de-airing pugmill. The use of a vacuum causes air pockets to explode and subsequent pugging from the vacuumed state
packs the particles together. Once through a de-airing pugmill
is said to equal two months of ageing.

Souring

Ageing is a physical action. Souring is rather different as it
involves organic action. Bacteria in the clay break down the
organic matter and multiply. The decomposition releases amino
acids which flocculate the fine particles. In doing so they create
a colloidal gel. The clay turns a blue-grey colour inside due to
the bacterial action which uses oxygen and reduces the oxide
content of the clay, and it begins to smell. This is why it is called
souring.

A clay which smells like rotting vegetation is therefore prized
and portions are added to other clays to spread the growth. A
clay kept especially for handles should always smell. It will be the
same clay as the body clay but will have extra strength. A gardener's

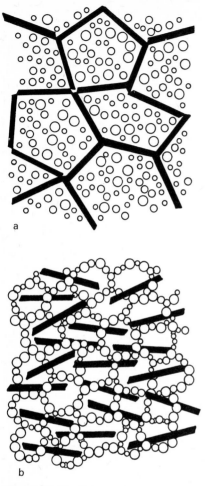

Fig 22 (a) Kaolinite particles are attracted at the edges and build a weak flocculated structure. (b) Colloidal particles are flocculated in a fine strong structure which supports kaolinite particles.

soil disinfectant which encourages bacteria can be added to clays to promote this action, but it should be added in a much diluted form or else it will kill the bacteria. Yeast and sugar are also used.

The full potential of a given clay body is achieved by ageing and souring together. The change in alkalinity/acidity of the soluble environment develops a progressively stronger structure.

The thixotropy which gives the clay the strength to hold together depends upon the flocculation of some of the particles. When these particles are flocculated they are attracted to each other and held by mutual forces of attraction. In the case of the hexagonal plate-like kaolinite particles the forces of attraction are strongest on the edges (Figure 22a). This makes them form an open lattice structure or card-house structure within which coarser non-clay particles and the much finer particles are held.

A non-aged clay where the particles are compacted into relatively coarse grains (including those of the montmorillonite bentonite which are capable of much finer dispersion) will be flocculated in this way. At a given consistency e.g. that considered suitable for throwing, the adhesion is just sufficient to allow the kaolinite particles to hold on the edges. The edges of the plates being below colloidal size the forces of attraction are greatest here. The faces of the shapes are too large to have forces strong enough to attract each other. If this clay feels too stiff for working i.e. there is too much resistance to pressure, the addition of more water loosens the lattice structure. The edges of the particles lose their grip and the clay ruptures and sticks to anything but itself.

The power of attraction between particles is related to their size and shape and the alkalinity/acidity of the water. The non-aged clay just described would have most of its particles of about the kaolinite size. The maximum flocculation for this size of particle occurs when the acidity is relatively weak.

Most clays contain montmorillonite and other minerals whose particles can be below colloidal size. Tests comparing kaolinite and montmorillonite show that the degree of acidity that promotes the maximum flocculation of kaolinite does not flocculate montmorillonite. (U. Hofmann). This solution has a cleaving action on montmorillonite layers creating even smaller particles and forcing water between them.

A change in the alkalinity/acidity (pH value) of the water brings the mutual attraction of finer particles into operation. A more acidic environment brings montmorillonite particles closer so that bonds are formed. The lattice structure created by montmorillonite is stronger than that of kaolinite. Also included amongst the finer, colloidal particles of clay constituents are minerals with particles and crystals of different shapes. These are rod-shapes and spheres which are capable of strong attraction over all their surface. Their fields of force for their size are so strong as to make them weightless.

Increased acidity brings these particles close together, and their mutual attraction holds them together in an extremely strong lattice. This is a colloidal gel. The lattice is quickly rejoined if broken under pressure. This is the ideal thixotropy (Figure 22b). This relatively increased acidity is brought about by the release of amino acids into the clay by the bacterial action which occurs in souring.

The degree of acidity which creates the colloidal gel destroys the flocculation of the kaolinite, especially the larger grains. These lose their optimum attraction and begin to repel each other, even when closely packed. This decreases the friction of the larger clay particles i.e. the resistance to pressure is less. The large particles then slide easily across one another. The strong lattice of the colloidal gel however, holds each new shape as it is formed.

The conclusion can be drawn, therefore, that ageing and souring work together progressively. Ageing reduces particle size and souring changes the alkalinity to acid, promoting flocculation of the colloidal particles.

The progess is simulated in the production of clay by high-speed blunging with deflocculants followed by flocculation for filter-pressing, and de-air pugging. The slow natural process probably achieves the optimum thixotropy better because the bacterial action takes other factors, pressure and temperature, into account, creating a fine balance of conditions to give the correct gel at the correct time.

Sand and grog
The thrower may add non-plastic grains (sand and grog) to his clay to improve 'bite' and enable him to 'lift' the clay better. He will adjust the coarseness and amount until he feels he has an effective balance of this texture with the plasticity of the clay.

Different forming processes demand different kinds of workability. In particular, plasticity, when not required is a decided disadvantage because of the attendant high shrinkage rate and warping problems. This is most apparent in making flatware. Clays for making tiles and large slab-ware are based on coarser clays with a high percentage addition of sand or grog. As much as forty per cent grog is viable with a forming process which allows plasticity to be disregarded.

Grog is ground fired body added to clays to provide a proportion of already fired and often refractory material. It provides texture, both tactile and visual, along with bite for better control in forming. It is an opener which helps the clay to dry uniformly and, because already fired, it proportionately cuts down the overall shrinkage and hence any tendency to crack or warp. Most grogs are fireclay fired to at least 1300°C (2372°F), and therefore more refractory than the body to which they are added. The word grog is sometimes used in a less specific way to mean any opener, thus embracing sand, quartz, feldspar, raw fireclay and even sawdust.

Sometimes a soft-fired grog is used. The advantage of this is that it is very porous and useful in the tempering of very sticky clays and in promoting quick drying.

If the soft grog is the same body as that to which it is added it is called pitchers. The advantage of using pitchers is that the working character of the body can be altered for various sizes and types of ware, but the fired result is the same. The same glazes and firing schedules can therefore be used.

Grogs are graded by screening and given a mesh size. Two numbers such as 30/60 mean that all will pass through a 30's mesh but not a 60's mesh. 60/Dust means that all will pass through a 60's mesh and some particles may be exceedingly small.

The foregoing considerations of workability have all aimed at producing an ideal clay from the making point of view. The choice of materials to give the required final fired effect makes other demands which must be compatible.

4 Drying

Technically, drying is the establishment of equilibrium moisture content between object and air. Wet clay dries by wetting the air around it. When the air holds as much water as the clay, the drying ceases.

Clay can therefore only dry out up to a point which is determined by the atmosphere.

Three factors are involved in drying: temperature, which encourages evaporation; humidity of surrounding air; and the movement of the air past the surface, thereby replacing saturated air with drier air. In simple terms the conditions which are good for drying washing out of doors are good for drying pots, whether these conditions are natural or created in the workshop. When barometric pressure is high, the atmosphere can hold more water than when pressure is low. The most effective conditions could cause unequal drying at rims and handles. This results in warpage and cracking and must be avoided by sheltering the pots or slowing down the drying rate. Pots will need to be turned around and over to even out the effects of sun and wind.

The theory of dewatering

The easiest way to understand the theory of drying and to relate this to pot making is to consider it as two stages. The first stage is the removal of the water of plasticity, and the second stage is the removal of the pore water. The leatherhard state is the dividing point.

The enlarged sections, figures 23a — d, show the stages in detail. Figures a and b are the first stage and figures c and d are the second stage.

Figure 23a is a plastic clay. Here there is some friction caused by the suction seal of the water between particles. The particles can be moved past one another using the water as lubricant. In contrast, figure 23b shows leatherhard clay in which the particles have physical contact and friction.

At this point it should be realized that each clay particle has a surrounding layer of water which is firmly attached. In the diagrams, this is shown as a white border. This is part of the bound water content. The water is held there by the hydroxyl groups and unsatisfied valencies of the clay crystal structure. In comparison with the clay crystal, it is a very thin layer — a few molecules in thickness. On the finest clay particle this would mean about a hundredth of the diameter, yet this layer provides a lubricated cushion. In leatherhard clay, as shown in figure 23b, these cushions are touching and thus provide a 'solid' state. The anchorage is by molecular attraction but there is still sufficient 'loose' water on the outside of the layer to act as a lubricant. Leatherhard clay can be reshaped by strong pressure without completely rupturing the whole piece of clay.

Clay can only dry where the water can evaporate at the surface. (The clay surface is shown at the top of the diagrams).

Fig 23 (a to d) As the lubricating water dries out, the particles come into contact. Most shrinkage occurs between plastic and leatherhard stages. The pore water then dries out and the particles share the bound water layers.

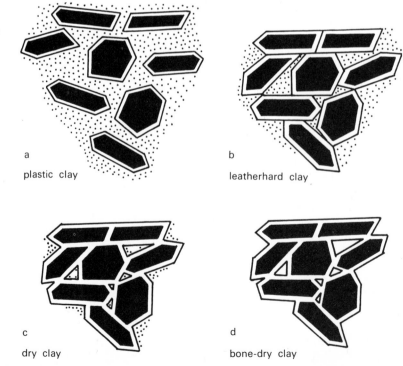

a
plastic clay

b
leatherhard clay

c
dry clay

d
bone-dry clay

Water migrates from the centre of the clay through the pores to the surface. As the gaps between the particles close, it becomes increasingly difficult for the water to migrate — it can do so only by a system of substitutions along the bound water layers or by circuitous routes via pores that are still linked. The drying process therefore slows down considerably.

Figure 23c represents air-dried clay. This is the furthest dry state possible in the open air. The tiniest pores are still filled with water but the large pores have drained and contain only a meniscus of water held by capillary action. The bound layer of water around each clay particle is theoretically reduced to its minimum. This is seen where two particles 'touch'. The particles now share the same layer and it is only two or three molecules thick. The whole mass of clay is now solid and cannot be reshaped without rupturing the bonds between the particles and thus breaking the clay.

Final stages

The size of pore which is able to retain its water is determined by the humidity of the air and the atmospheric pressure. The amount of water in air-dried clay therefore varies from day-to-day. Not only do the pores dry out to this determined point, but also those pores which were empty fill up to this point by taking water from the air. This is called readsorption. Most clays can withstand these daily adjustments of water content without ill effect. However if clay is dried thoroughly and then allowed to readsorb moisture, a slight expansion takes place which causes cracks with some clays in certain sections. Therefore if pots are dried on a kiln top they should be fired while they are still warm rather than after allowing them to cool again, especially if conditions are humid.

Figure 23d represents bone-dry clay. This state occurs in the early stages of firing, after the water-smoking period, and is considered as existing from 120°C (248°F) up to the ceramic change at 600°C (1112°F). In bone-dry clay the pore water has gone but the bound water remains to be eventually driven off in the ceramic change. The pore water must be driven off carefully because there are few passages through which it can escape to the surface.

Shrinkage

An important effect of drying is shrinkage. Shrinkage, or rather unequal shrinkage, is responsible for drying cracks and warpage.

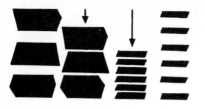

Fig 24. Fine clay shrinks more than coarse clay.

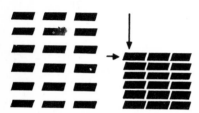

Fig 25. Alignment of particles creates greater shrinkage in one direction.

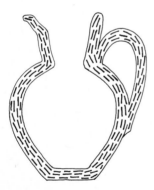

Fig 26. In a thrown pot wall the particles become aligned with their flat faces opposing the direction of forming pressures.

Figure 24 shows that fine clay will shrink more than coarse clay during drying. The fine clay also contains more water.

Figure 25 shows how a clay will shrink more in one direction than in the other when all the clay particles are lying flat upon one another. This situation arises in pots.

Clay particles position themselves with their flat faces opposing the direction of pressure. An extreme example of this is seen in compressed clays which have become shales. However in all potting use, the particles are being asked to rearrange their relative positions. Rolling and press-moulding lays the particles flat along the clay sheet. This gives strength. In kneading clay, the particles are pushed concentrically. This gives circular strength which is useful on the wheel and is further added to by the centring process. During opening of the clay in throwing, the base of the pot is compressed. This lays the particles flat across the base giving strength. It also makes the larger drying shrinkage through the thickness of the base rather than across the base. The firing shrinkage also follows this course (Figure 26).

Avoiding trouble
Where differently-made parts of a pot are joined, as in the case of a pulled handle attached to a thrown pot, the different patterns of clay particles present an unconformity. If these patterns are not modified by very thorough joining, stresses are set up at this point. In shrinking the unequal tensions may cause the clay to rupture. Thus the drying and shrinking may show up weak points or faults which were contained in the pot but not visible until this stage. This is why uniform drying is essential especially for pieces of complicated shape.

The loss of the slide effect from the water of plasticity between the particles makes the clay more brittle at dry stage than at leatherhard stage and therefore more susceptible to cracking and breakage.

Fine clay which has been burnished resists complete drying. Burnishing compacts the finest particles on the surface, closing the pores and trapping water inside. The drying of such ware must therefore be done more slowly at first and more thoroughly in the last stages.

Speed of drying

One sometimes needs to dry pots quickly, to meet deadlines or because a lot of raw pots can take up a lot of precious workshop space. There are times to be cautious and times when drying can be done speedily.

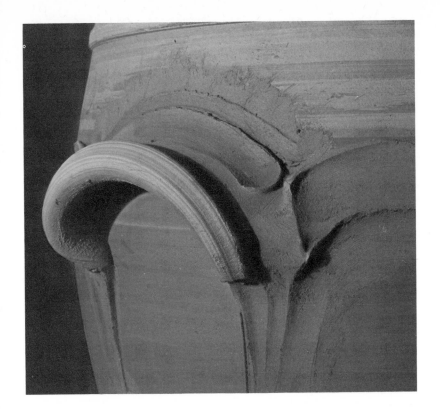

Fig 27. Thorough joining of handle to pot body prevents shrinkage cracks. *Bread crock by Michael Casson*

In a constant atmosphere the drying process slows down after the leatherhard stage. The particles are now touching and so further shrinkage is negligible. The danger period for shrinkage cracks is therefore from plastic state to leatherhard state. The most complicated shapes are the most vulnerable, partly because projecting parts will catch the moving air more than the main body, and also because of possible unconformity at joins. Even the simplest, strong shape of a globular pinch pot could warp where drying is one-sided. Caution is needed until the piece is beyond leatherhard stage. Where the section is thick much more time must be allowed for water to dry out from the centre.

From this point work can be dried quickly in the sun or on top of the kiln.

5 Slip

Dry clay is a hard material which can be turned into a plastic material by the addition of water. If still more water is added the stable state is lost and the mixture becomes a liquid. In general parlance, if the mixture contains lumps and liquid we call it a slurry but if we sieve it so that it is a creamy homogeneous mixture we call it a slip.

Slips are used to coat a clay for a number of reasons, e.g. for decoration, smooth surface and improved glaze fit. The most usual is to provide decoration. The slip is made from either a different colour of clay from the main body of the work or else the same clay with added colouring. A whole range of colours is possible and will be brightest if the starting point is a white clay. It is possible to darken slips by staining but not to lighten them. White-burning ball clay is a popular starting point for making decorative slips. The following are suggested maximum amounts of colouring oxides which, when added to a white clay, give full strength colours.

Chromium oxide	5%	grey-green
Cobalt oxide	5%	blue
Copper oxide	5%	green glazed, buff unglazed
Iron oxide	15%	cream to brown and black
Manganese dioxide	20%	browns

The brightest, clear colours require prepared stains added to a maximum of twenty per cent. Colour manufacturers offer blues, turquoises, greens, yellows, oranges, purples, reds and blacks.

The colour of any slip varies according to whether it is glazed or unglazed. If glazed, the composition of the covering glaze influences the colour produced. Generally speaking, glazes containing lead oxide give mellow rich colours while leadless

Fig 28. A leatherhard pot is dipped into slip to give it a smooth coating of a different colour.

41

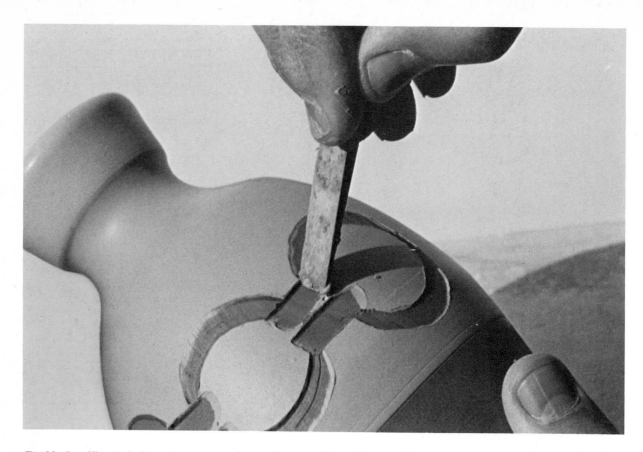

Fig 29. Sgraffito technique. A wooden tool is used to scrape away parts of the soft slip coating to reveal the body clay.

glazes sharpen the colours. Glazes give a depth to the colour whereas unglazed slips have a flat appearance and are never quite so bright. In all cases the prepared stains give more uniform colours because they are already stable combinations of colouring oxide and silica, alumina etc., in predetermined proportion. Colouring oxides, as opposed to stains, make their combination as the firing takes place and therefore vary.

Coloured slip can be dewatered to produce coloured clay. In fact this is the most practical way of producing a clay with uniform colouring which is required for ceramic jewellery, sprigging and inlay decorations.

Simple dips are the most direct way of decorating pottery with slip. Many rural potteries in the 18th and 19th centuries used a reddish clay which was probably also slightly sandy. By the use of a cream-coloured slip poured inside and poured out again a pot was given a light interior and one which when glazed gave a

smooth surface. The pot was often dipped mouth downwards into the slip at least over the rim giving accent to the rim and contrast to the darker body. Jugs were often dipped over the spout and front area with what is called a bib dip. The natural follow-on from this is to comb the slip layer with the fingers while it is still wet. This gives added contrast and simple motifs. Scratching away the slip coating when leatherhard or dry gives finer control for the drawing of imagery. The method is known as *sgraffito* from the Italian.

Wet slip is an inviting material to make patterns in because of its fresh and direct qualities. Running one colour of slip into a layer of another colour by the use of a nozzle is called trailing. It provides a most exciting decoration, both colourful and positive, which if covered with a shiny transparent glaze seems to sparkle with life.

To make a bucketful of slip, simply put water into a bucket

Fig 30. Lines of coloured slip are trailed into wet slip on a clay slab to produce a pattern of contrasted colours.

to about nine-tenths of the final amount required and add powdered clay, mixing it in until the slip is of correct thickness. The proportion of clay to water is different for each type of clay. A ball clay, for example, is able to absorb a large amount of water and so less clay is required than if one were using a coarser clay like fireclay. For a five litre bucketful of slip one requires approximately 4·5 litres of water and not less than 2·5 kilos and not more than 4·5 kilos of dry clay. Powder mixes in more quickly than dry lumps or broken pots. Large lumps could take a few days to slake down, so if the slip is required urgently, it is worthwhile crushing the lumps to powder before adding to the water. Colouring oxides or stains are added with the powder. The resulting mixed slurry is passed through a 60's mesh sieve to produce an homogeneous slip. More water can be added and stirred in if the slip is too thick so it is better to err on this side.

Slips made up from ball clay often thicken slightly after standing overnight. This is known as maturing. It involves the subdivision of the largest grains as water soaks between the agglomerated particles. More water can be added and stirred in. If a slip has been mixed up and it is too thin, allow it to settle and syphon or pour off some of the water before stirring it for use. Sometimes slips become thin and will not settle. This happens where slips contain materials with soluble content. These slips can be thickened with calcium chloride.

Problems of fit

Slip behaves like the clay from which it is made, in that it fires to the same colour and has the same overall shrinkage and vitrification range. Theoretically therefore, a slip should be capable of covering the same clay without any problems. In practice this is not always so because the slip, which is very wet, is applied to clay which is probably leatherhard. The water in the slip soaks into the leatherhard clay and the particles in the slip orientate to form a layered shell. This layered shell has differential shrinkage. In proportion it shrinks more in thickness than across its surface, with the result that it does not exactly fit the clay that it covers.

Occasionally this slight misfit of slip to clay results in loss of adhesion seen as flaking before or after biscuit firing and even after glaze firing. The slip can be helped towards a better fit by making it 'richer' so that it shrinks more. The simplest way to do this is to sieve it distinctly finer than the body. A 100's or 120's mesh usually suffices. Alternatively some highly plastic clay like ball clay can be added to the slip to increase its overall shrinkage rate. Loss of adhesion can also be the fault of the clay itself. Some clays are not sticky and so not join to themselves readily. Additions of vinegar to the slip sometimes improve stickiness but choice of a sticky clay for the slip is probably the better practice. Again a fine ball clay cannot be bettered.

Vitrifying slips

Shrinkage during the later stage of firing is dependent upon a clay's or slip's vitrification. A slip of different colour from the clay which it covers is sure to vitrify and shrink differently. Fortunately during vitrification the slip fuses itself on to the clay body thus improving adhesion. If flaking occurs and is diagnosed as insufficient fusion, the slip can be given extra vitrification by the addition of frit, feldspar or glaze. The amount of additive is found by trial, the maximum being about twenty per cent. At the raw stage slips which are vitrified in this way tend to be flakey and lack adhesion because they contain non-plastic (non-sticky) materials. The raw state adhesion is sacrificed for adhesion in the finished state. To overcome this some potters add glue (PVA, animal or vegetable) to their slips, but the whole balance is a compromise even so.

Vitrifying slips fuse themselves onto the clay during firing. Glazes are able to fuse themselves onto these slips more readily than on to refractory clays. Thus the layer provided by a vitrifying slip creates an artificial body-glaze layer. When a vitrifying slip is used for this purpose — to provide a smoother surface and one intermediate in fusion between body and glaze — it is known as a buffer. It is called an engobe if it introduces colour also.

By becoming half glaze a slip loses its opacity. Light slips covering dark bodies allow some of the body colour to show through attractively or annoyingly, according to what was expected. Slips strongly coloured by cobalt, iron and manganese oxides bleed into the glaze in an attractive way.

Slip glazes

A slip which contains around twenty per cent flux or thirty per cent frit comes into the category of a fusible slip or slip glaze. That is, when fired without a covering of glaze to temperatures above $1200°C$ ($2192°F$) it is difficult to identify the result as a product of a slip or clay because it is more like a glaze or glass. There is nothing really surprising in this since all clays have their melting points. Fireclay, the kiln itself, would melt to produce a glass in the region of $1700°$ to $1800°C$ ($3092°$ to $3272°F$). Clays which melt at pottery temperatures can be used as glazes when applied as slips to raw clay. They are called slip-glazes.

Slip glazes are prepared by combining fluxes and other glaze materials with clays. Examples are whiting, dolomite, feldspars, frits of all kinds and wood ash. Wood ash is particularly popular because it gives interesting depth of quality. Different woods give variously speckled effects, often yellow or brown from iron impurities, and with crystalline surfaces. The friable nature of the other fluxes produces a flakey loose-fitting layer inhibiting the natural stickiness of the clay, but the fibrous wood ash assists adhesion during drying. Slip glazes produced in this way deflocculate themselves over a period of weeks as the soluble alkalis dissolve from the wood ash, feldspar and frits. The slip becomes too fluid so that an insufficient layer is coated on the ware. The addition of an acid (vinegar will do) corrects this and thickens the slip and the coating. It also helps the slip coat to dry quickly.

Natural slip-glazes occur as estuarine muds, the most famous being Albany slip. This is surprisingly low in fluxes, about thirteen per cent, but is also low in the refractory alumina. It contains a high proportion of iron oxide which encourages fusion above $1200°C$ ($2192°F$) and gives the resulting glaze its rich brown colour. It is usual to assist fusion with feldspar.

Another famous slip-glaze is that of the Roman Samian ware or *terra sigillata*. This is a red clay ware with a glossy surface fired between $900°$ and $1000°C$ ($1652°$ and $1832°F$). The glaze is a thin layer of extremely fine clay particles, possibly with added red iron oxide. To separate these sub-micron particles from the clay it is necessary to mix the clay with a large amount of water, add deflocculants, repeatedly decant the finest suspensions, and finally dry the thin slip to usable density.

Casting slips

In slip casting, a porous mould is filled with slip. The mould is usually plaster of Paris and composed of two or more parts fitted together. The slip remains in the mould for a period of minutes during which time some of the water is absorbed, thus building up a layer of clay against the wall of the mould. The excess slip is poured away and when the cast has stiffened the mould is dismantled. The resulting hollow form is dried, fettled and fired in the usual way.

Any slip will work but for maximum efficiency a special slip is prepared. The process dictates four considerations. The slip must be sufficiently fluid to run freely and fill all details; having filled every corner of the mould it must take an accurate impression; it must be sufficiently permeable to allow water to

pass through it as it builds up into a clay layer against the wall of
the mould; and lastly the newly formed cast, although still wet,
must remain firm until it has hardened sufficiently to be removed
from the mould.

To pour freely into every corner of the mould a slip must be
very fluid. But the simple addition of water to give fluidity
presents too much water for the mould to absorb and a firm cast
cannot be achieved. To create a slip which has both a high clay
content and a high fluidity we make use of the phenomenon
called deflocculation. By the addition of suitable chemicals called
deflocculants, electrolytes or, popularly, alkalis, the clay particles
are made to repel each other and the slip is rendered extremely
fluid.

Fig 31. Casting slip gives a strong
and firm cast which parts cleanly
from the mould.

47

Fig 32 (a) card-stack structure (b) card-house structure of clay particles give a dense compacted clay and a permeable clay respectively.

Fig 33. Clay particles of large electrostatic charge successfully repel each other, thus creating highly fluid slips.

Deflocculation

Clay particles are flat hexagonal plates. If these plates lie side by side or on top of one another in a flat way it is possible to fit more in a given volume of water than if the plates are determined to come to rest at angles to each other. These two situations are called card-stack structure and card-house structure (Figure 32).

Small clay particles in suspension in water attract one another by individual gravity, causing drag which inhibits the flow of the slip. But if the clay particles are persuaded to repel one another instead of attracting one another, then a more fluid slip is created. This is achieved by the addition of deflocculants which increase a particle's electrostatic charge. When each particle has a similar large charge it repels every other particle.

These charges are concentrated at the edges of the plate-like particles and the zone of repulsion is in reality only small. However the effect of the charges is as if the zone were a protective figure-of-eight in section. This is diagrammatized in Figure 33. The repulsion zones ensure that the particles cannot come into contact and so there is no friction to hinder fluidity. Even in high concentrations of particles, that is, in a slip containing a large amount of clay and a small amount of water, the particles refuse to meet and continue to repel one another. They position themselves in the most economical use of the volume which is the card-stack structure. A slip in this state is described as deflocculated.

The reverse of the action just described is a combination of high friction (attraction and physical abrasion) and card-house structure. This gives a viscous slip which has an open pore structure. Such a slip is flocculated. Most natural clays give slips which are nearer to this state than that of deflocculation but since domestic water softeners and the solubles from wood ash and frits are deflocculatory it is impossible to talk of a 'normal' slip. The possible range is from fully deflocculated to fully flocculated. For slip casting the slip must be near to the fully deflocculated state but with sufficient open structure still evident to allow the water to pass through the build-up of clay on the wall of the mould. A fully deflocculated slip would create a waterproof layer.

Clay particles have an ability to set firm once they have been forced into contact by the withdrawal of the lubricating layer of water. This is the property 'thixotropy' discussed in chapter 3. It is unaltered by some deflocculants but destroyed by others. The deflocculants which destroy this useful property bring other advantages so a balance of the two types is used. In practice this means that sodium carbonate (soda ash) is used to increase the power of the charges and sodium silicate to increase both the power and the number of charges. Sodium carbonate has little effect upon existing thixotropy but sodium silicate decreases it.

It is normal practice to work to a density around 34 oz pint U.K., 28 oz pint U.S. or 170 grams per 100cc. Recipes for casting slips will be found in Appendix 4.

Unlike throwing clay, casting slip is at its best when freshly mixed. Slip cannot be stored indefinitely but can be kept for about twenty days if the storage tank is non-corrosive and reasonably airtight.

6 Preparation

Pottery making is a complete craft. More than with any other modern craft it can be practised through the complete cycle from raw materials to finished product. This is a situation to rejoice in. If your aim is to carry out the full cycle from the beginning, there may at times seem to be hours of laborious preparation. The reward is that you are in a position to choose and design the full character of your work. Experience with clay makes you aware of its importance as the prime determining factor.

The highest degree of plasticity and strength is required for throwing since that is the most fluent and fast way of shaping. Pressing on moulds and jigger-jolley benefit from plasticity but strength is not essential. Slabbed pots need a fairly plastic clay where the pieces are curved, twisted or wrapped around a mould or in a free-form style. The formal box construction type of slab pot needs a clay tempered with sand or grog to avoid the stresses of warping and shrinking which this kind of shape does not easily accommodate.

The slower processes of coiling and pinching allow the use of coarser, poorer clays. Being more adaptable, completely individual methods, the design can be continuously modified to use and exhibit the quality of the clay. Therefore a relatively weak, coarser material or very short porcelain clay can be pinched carefully into a pot shape although it would be quite unusable by any other method.

Pockets of clay of perfect consistency and ideal composition for a particular product can be found. This proves that the preparation of clay for working is a natural process of events. All that the potter does is to simulate nature's ideas, accelerate them and emphasize one or another to produce the clay he requires. It is important to appreciate this and to try to work with nature rather than against it.

A few clays are suitable for potting as dug from the ground. Some are potentially good clays but require preparation. It is all too easy to assume that the earliest potters used their clay 'as dug'. The exceedingly coarse nature of some of the bodies of Bronze Age pottery might lead one to think that no selection or preparation was carried out. However a closer study of primitive pottery proves this to be wrong. The pottery made today by people classified as stone age shows a remarkable understanding of the practical necessity of clay preparation, even if the technology is not understood. These people work with nature.

Anthropologists have sometimes expressed amazement when observing that a woman will take the trouble to remove sand from a clay only to add sand from another locality. It is hardly surprising that the potter could not explain dunting! Nevertheless she does know that one sand is good for the flame-proof body whereas another is not.

A typical preparation sequence to produce a throwing clay from a raw clay would be:

1. weathering
2. blunging
3. sieving
4. settling
5. dewatering
6. wedging
7. storage
8. preparation for the wheel.

Not all clays will improve by weathering, only those which have plastic potential. A study of the geological origin of the clay will help to identify the clay type. A clay in its first stages of disintegration may take a hundred or a thousand years to become weathered. It may take millions of years before weathering can change ordered kaolinite to a fully plastic clay.

At the other end of the scale are clays that once were fully plastic but by pressure and drying have now become compacted again and consist of large grains. These grains are vulnerable to weathering so that a clay of this sort will show surprising disintegration after one year's weathering. These clays are rock-like fireclays, marl shales etc. After millions of years in the earth as rocks, they weather to plastic clays in a few years, the hardest taking perhaps twenty.

An important agent in disintegration is the frost. Water alone will slowly penetrate the clay grain that has plastic potential but frost greatly accelerates the process. Water expands as it freezes, causing the gap between the particles to widen and flood with water upon thawing. Once water has entered one end of a potential gap it drives a wedge inwards by the alternate actions of freezing and thawing. Following the frost, the particles are only loosely held by water bonds. Now the physical action of rain beating upon the clay is sufficient to move the particles apart.

Secondary clays that have been transported by water, ground and tossed about in rivers and finally allowed to rest below a lake, tend to be plastic. However if these clays have also dried out, been compressed or otherwise dehydrated, they will tend to have lost their plasticity. The particles will be packed tightly together to form large grains. From this one learns that, even on the smaller scale of the workshop, it is a retrograde step to allow intended plastic clay to dry out at any stage. For a clay to realize its full plastic potential, it requires water between the particles. Clays which are weathering should therefore be kept wet.

Weathering can be simulated by blunging. A whole winter's weathering can be achieved in ten minutes of high speed blunging. This literally forces the particles to collide with shattering impact. At this shock instant the water seepage is rapid. Blunging is done in an octagonal or hexagonal tank with a central vertical shaft. On this shaft is fastened a number of radial blades or paddles. These are set at an angle so that, when the shaft rotates, the blades force the mixture downwards. The resulting creamy slurry is run out of the tank by a tap at the bottom. It can then be sieved, settled etc. A recent development is centrifugal blunging which uses a small, high-speed impellor at the base of the tank.

Small amounts of raw clay can be left to soak and then are most quickly dealt with by hand. Larger amounts need either a paddle, which is a flattened stick, or a dolly, which is a perforated disc set on the end of a stick. The underside of the disc has a few sharp dowels protruding which break up the solids as the dolly is raised and lowered. The holes flush the mixture to mix it. A power drill with a long rod with a loop at the end is very effective.

Weathering also allows soluble salts to be washed away. It is true that blunging will also achieve this. However there is the point that during weathering an amount of chemical decomposition takes place. For the most part this decomposition and solution is desirable, but an end product is calcium sulphate which, if not washed away, causes scumming. Chemical correctives can be added at the blunging stage to complete decomposition and precipitate the salts as harmless compounds.

After all this treatment, some clays may be found to be too plastic and sticky. These clays are difficult to handle but improve in workability by the addition of some non-plastic material. As a general rule, the fine non-plastics decrease the plasticity more

Fig 34. A 30 cm octagonal blunger manufactured by Gosling and Gatensbury Ltd and marketed by Harrison Mayer Ltd. (*Photo supplied by the makers.*)

than the coarse ones. It is sufficient to add grogs and sand at the kneading or pugging stage, but powders must be added at the blunging stage.

Powders, even wet powders, do not seem to mix thoroughly. They create agglomerate grains of their own if added to the clay at its plastic stage. Such powders are china clay and quartz flour. It may seem time-wasting to add these to the suspension, only to sieve them and dewater them, but they do not seem to mix otherwise. It is of course pointless to add material of a size that will later be held back by a sieve.

You can obtain some idea of what a raw clay contains by a simple experiment. You require a glass bottle that will hold about a pint. This is half-filled with water and about half a teaspoonful of the clay is added. It can be added in any convenient state, but the idea is to get it into suspension by vigorously shaking the bottle. When the clay is in suspension, the bottle can be almost filled with water and shaken again to mix the suspension. The bottle is then put at a slight angle.

As the water comes to a standstill, the heavy material immediately settles and progressive sedimentation of different grain sizes follows. If there is sufficient plastic clay present to make a suitable potting clay, the mixture should remain completely cloudy for at least two hours. In fact it will take at least a day to completely settle.

The slight tilt on the bottle emphasizes the sediments into indentifiable layers against one side of the glass. If the test is carried out on a window sill the light shining through the bottle helps to identify the particles. A magnifying glass can even be used through the side of the bottle.

Bentonite can be added to a clay which has insufficient of the ultra-fine particles. This would be a clay that settled completely in four or five hours. Two per cent of bentonite is usually sufficient.

With a locally dug clay it is often necessary to take out unwanted material. This material may be large like twigs, roots, leaves and stones, or it may be small like sand or shale.

Large objects can be sorted by hand — a process used by primitive potters and one which does not take as long as you might think. If the clay is in plastic state, small pellets are broken off and squashed between finger and thumb. Large unwanted pieces are felt and removed. Some carbonaceous matter present as hair roots is often advantageous to plasticity. It will certainly help in the souring.

A larger problem is unwanted sand and shale. Weathered shales are often a nuisance in this respect, containing a lot of flat slatey pieces that do not reconstitute as clay.

The only way to get rid of this unwanted material is by turning the clay into a very thin slurry with water. In this state pieces of wood and carbonaceous matter often float and can be skimmed off. Very large and heavy material sinks and can be left behind in the container. Finer sand and shale is removed by sieving.

A 60's mesh gives a good general potting clay. Some potters prefer finer clays and use an 80's or 100's mesh, but take the suspension through a 20's or 40's mesh first. Too much coarse material might otherwise accumulate and tear the finer mesh. A brush should be used sparingly. There is no point in forcing material through the mesh because this is unlikely to be clay material. A brush can be used to keep the mesh clear. A vibrating mesh is the best method. The use of a very thin or watery suspension helps to break the clay content into its finest particles. Overnight soaking before sieving will help to reach plasticity potential and will help the suspension to flow through the mesh without clogging.

Some clays will not settle after this process. The addition of some acid to the water will increase the settling rate but fine clays, and these are the plastic clays, will always settle slowly. This is a good sign. Two or four days is not too long to wait for a good clay. The use of a test as previously described will give some indication of the mesh size to select, and the time required for decanting the suspension from the first heavy sediment.

Clays which contain unwanted material which is as fine as the wanted clay can be refined by levigation. The process involves the use of the different densities of the clay and the unwanted material. The heavier material of higher density sinks in water quicker than the lighter material. On a large scale, timed settling and elutriation are also used. The process is sometimes necessary to remove sand specking from light-coloured clays. Porcelain bodies are sometimes refined in this way to get the maximum plasticity and purity. After settling and syphoning, the resulting thick slip is poured into drying troughs, on to absorbent boards, on to a heated floor, or just left in the open air to dry. Frequent attention is required to forestall any tendency to dry out too much at the edges.

On a large scale, which is anything requiring more than a hundredweight of plastic clay daily, a filter press is used. A deflocculant gives the extra fluidity for sieving. The clay is returned to its stiffer and more permanent state by a flocculant. This thick slip is pumped under pressure or suction into a series of demountable boxes whose faces are made of a permeable, fine, strong cloth. The water passes through the cloths and the clay is held back to produce a 'cake'.

The 'cakes' of clay may then be stored carefully to be aged and soured for as long as possible. If needed urgently they can be prepared for immediate use, though even a few days ageing will improve the quality noticeably. Additions of sand or grog can be made at this stage as the clay is compressed by wedging and kneading or in a pugmill. A pugmill mechanizes the handwork of wedging and kneading; knives rotate on a central shaft and force the clay through a tapering barrel and out through a compressing nozzle. Individual potters use horizontal pugmills for small amounts and vertical pugmills for larger amounts. A de-airing pugmill gives greater compression. It first shreds the clay and then subjects it to a vacuum, the air pockets explode and the air is extracted. The clay is then re-united and compressed.

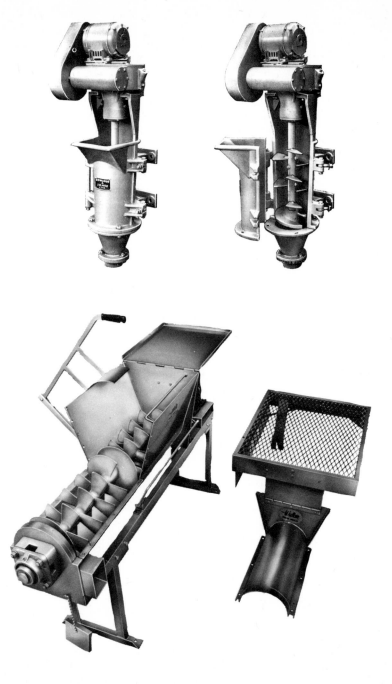

Fig 35. A vertical pugmill made by Edwards and Jones Ltd, Stoke-on-Trent. (*Photo supplied by the makers.*)

Fig 36. The Walker Mixer/Pugmill produces ready-to-use clay from dry powder or hard scraps. (*Photo supplied by Walker James Co. Inc, Duluth, Minnesota.*)

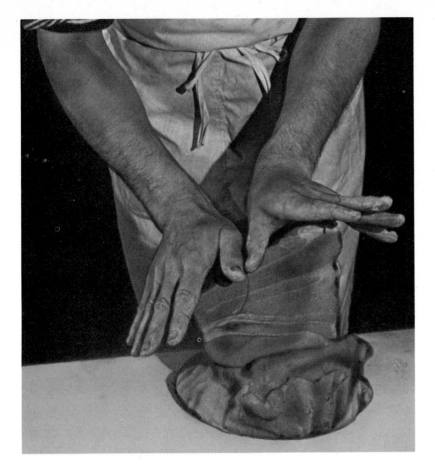

Fig 37. Wedging. The clay lump is sliced and one half is turned and thrown forcefully down on the other.

Pugging achieves some mixing of clay consistency but is more important for its effect upon compression. De-airing is necessary for industrial processes using fine but less plastic clays. At the other end of the working scale the de-aired clay is sometimes considered too dense or 'tight' by the hand thrower or modeller.

When preparing by hand, some potters use wedging as an initial mixing process and employ kneading for most of the conditioning of the clay. Some wedge only and some knead only: it depends upon the potter, his strength and the condition and type of clay.

In wedging, a conveniently sized lump of clay is thrown down on to the wedging bench. This is a stoutly built strong table about seventy cm. high. The lump of clay is thrown down to form a wedge shape with the wide end towards the potter. This end half is cut off with a wire, lifted, turned over and brought down to meet the other half with force. The whole lump is lifted, knocked on to the bench to regain its lump shape and thrown down to start the process again. The process is repeated fifty times or so until the clay is thoroughly mixed and compressed. Air bubbles are expelled where they lie close to a cut.

Kneading also mixes and compresses the clay and expels air bubbles by an action which rolls the clay upon itself, spreading and refolding it. The desired amount of clay is taken with hands close together and a part of it is pressed against the rest. The action is repeated with a slight progression. Two styles are known: they are ram's head or bull's head kneading which is the European method, and the spiral or shell kneading which is Oriental. The names describe the shapes produced by the actions. Kneading is often done as a specific preparation of weighed amounts immediately before using the clay. The close contact also gives the potter that vital information on the exact nature

Fig 38. Ram's head kneading. A large lump of clay is worked under both hands to mix and fold it.

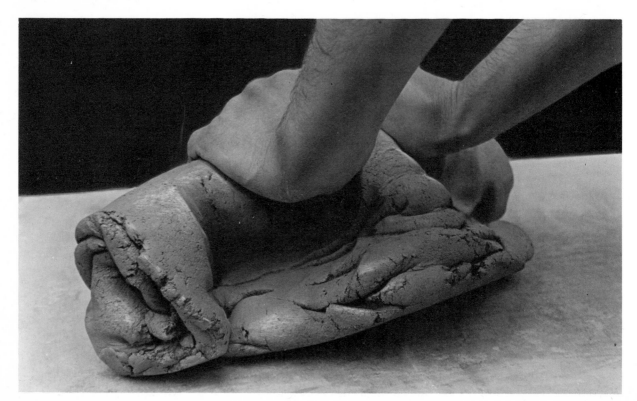

and quality of the material he is about to use.

Most plastic clays are stored in a slightly overwet condition. This assists ageing. Therefore plastic clay often requires a slight dewatering before use which is achieved by wedging and kneading on a slightly absorbent bench. If the clay is too soft, it may be necessary to use a very absorbent plaster block or asbestos board first to achieve correct moisture content. Alternatively, arches of clay left on a board outside in a breeze quickly stiffen and can be wedged and kneaded. Clay which has required much in the way of this late dewatering does not reach its maximum plasticity without a further rest in storage.

Clay that is too stiff can be remixed with water in a pugmill, a reconstituter popularly called a dough mixer, or by hand. It is a laborious process by hand but can be done by cutting the clay into slabs, poking holes in the slabs, and adding water or slurry before sandwiching. The lump is kneaded a little, wedged and kneaded again. This clay too will benefit from storage.

Clay which has dried out completely as scrapped pots or the

Fig 39. Spiral kneading. The top of the lump is pushed down by the right hand to fold and compress it.

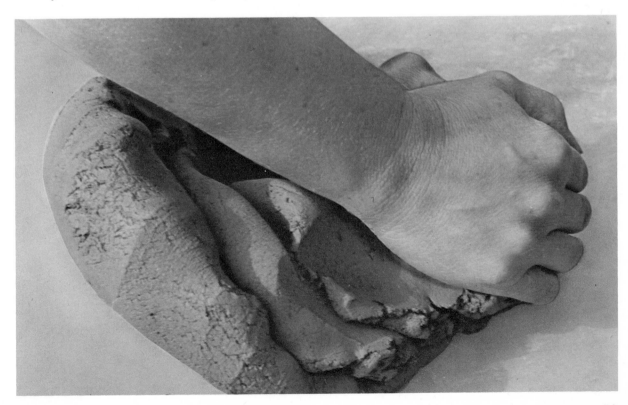

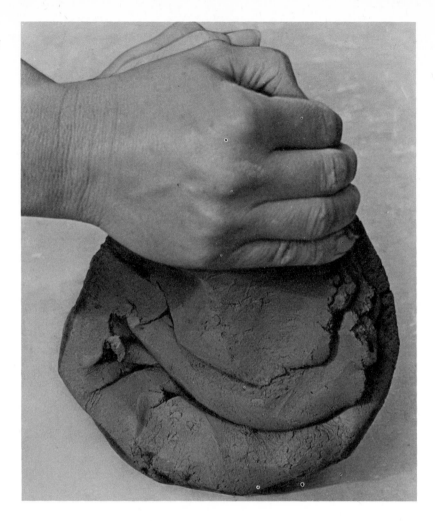

edges of clay which is dewatering should be resoaked if possible. This is the only way to achieve full plastic potential.

From the point of view of its fired properties the clay is mixed for its density or vitrification at a given temperature, for final colour under or without a glaze, for textural effects and, with ovenware or flame-proof ware, for its resistance to thermal shock.

The full science of making ware with the capacity of withstanding thermal shock is largely a matter of glazing and firing, and outside our scope here. The general principle at the clay stage is to use a clay which does not contain free silica and will not be very dense when fired. To cut down on the amount of expansion/contraction it must suffer, a high proportion of a refractory grog is added.

A body for raku firing is an extreme example of this. Usually a very coarse, refractory mixture is prepared.

To give a pleasant black or brown speckle to an uninteresting-looking clay, you can add coarse iron spangles (magnetic iron oxide) or coarse manganese dioxide — the iron speckle is more effective in a reduction firing. In a pale stoneware body one can use a dark, low firing red clay grog which will melt to give glossy brown spots.

Special coloured clays can be made either by dewatering from slip or by kneading oxide into clay. The slip method is used where completely uniform colouring is necessary. Colouring clay in this way can be expensive and the oxides used flux the clay and lower its firing temperature. Small amounts can be very effectively used in the inlay technique.

Egyptian paste is a special mixture which gives the beautiful, glossy bright turquoise blue of Egyptian beads. It contains soluble salts which dry out through the clay and deposit a coating on the surface, thereby providing a glaze.

7 Buying

A list of suppliers will be found as Appendix 1.
Clay is no longer 'cheap dirt'. By refinement and classification it has become an expensive commodity. Clays and bodies for named wares, e.g. stoneware, are mostly marketed in plastic state ready-wrapped in polythene to prevent drying out. A convenient size for handling and stacking is twenty or twenty-five kilos. Raw clays, e.g. ball clays, are usually in powder form, sometimes described as air floated, which means that the dried powder has been separated from the heavier pieces by blown air. Shredded clay is in dry or leatherhard pieces about the size of dried peas. Lump clay as dug may sometimes be purchased.

The names which suppliers have traditionally used for their clays have grown into a colourful collection of terms, some logical, some curious. Two or three words usually convey the most relevant information but they may be drawn from a variety of aspects. Earthenware, stoneware or porcelain refer to firing properties. Colours red, grey or black probably describe the raw clay, but white, ivory and buff may mean the fired colour. Texture when indicated as fine or coarse can be misleading as industrially-based suppliers are pre-disposed to fine clays. The original purpose of the clay is shown in wad, crank and school clay. The most picturesque names arise from their sources in the quarry as 'Brook's bottom vein', or from affection; 'Tough Tom' was a particularly workable red clay which could be relied on to improve shorter clays. 'St. Thomas's Body' refers simply to the school which first requested this blend.

Clay, body and paste

There is a difference between the terms 'clay' and 'body' by general use. As a general term, clay embraces all materials that are clay-like including bentonite. Specifically it means the natural material as dug or with reasonable refinement by removal of stones and large-grained sand. But as soon as we begin to add to a clay or blend one clay with another we create a body. A body is therefore produced with a particular end in view and has been blended or composed to give it specific working or fired properties. Thus most clays offered for sale in plastic state and described as containing a particular grog making them suitable for a particular process and ware are probably bodies.

The point is not without relevance because it is well to be aware, for example, how the high plasticity might have been achieved and whether the claim of good glaze fit is attributable to an addition of cristobalite or the natural balance of oxides. Bodies for some very specialized productions like bone china contain little clay and are rarely suitable for hand working. They are used in casting processes or pressings and are correctly described as pastes.

Fig 41. A nineteenth century earthenware tyg using the plasticity of the clay in richly looped and roped handles. H. 18cm.

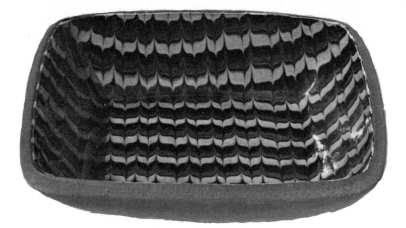

Fig 42. An ovenproof pressed dish made of porous earthenware and decorated with slip by Penny Barron. L. 20cm.

Ware names

Earthenware is pottery or modelling in which the fired clay is porous. A covering glaze, if used, provides a waterproof layer and decoration. The simplest division of all pottery into earthenware and stoneware can be done on the criterion of porosity using five per cent as the dividing line. Usually the firing temperature is also considered since this affects porosity and the glazes which can be used. Stoneware clay can be used as earthenware clay if it is used at temperatures below that at which it vitrifies. On the other hand many earthenware clays deform rapidly above stated firing ranges and therefore are unsuitable for stoneware. The earthenware range is up to 1200°C (2192°F) with most clays being fired in the 1050° to 1100°C range (1922° to 2012°F).

Red earthenware clay is often a natural refined clay. Terracotta refers more to the fired colour. In the raw state the clay varies from red-brown to grey. Cane clay for making straw-coloured earthenware is a refined fireclay. Buff clays which give deep cream colours when glazed or buff-pinks unglazed are often the stoneware clays used as earthenware.

White and cream earthenwares are produced from specially-blended bodies. These contain china clay for whiteness, ball clay for plasticity, possibly feldspar to create strength through vitrification, flint for whiteness and hardness, and probably cristobalite to improve glaze fit. The whitest bodies tend to be short. The more plastic the body the creamier its fired colour because the ball clay which gives plasticity and strength invariably contains some iron.

Stoneware is either non-porous (dense) or of low porosity (under five per cent). The slightly porous is the stronger. There are natural stoneware clays sometimes referred to as twice-removed ball clays or coloured ball clays. They are grey in colour, pinkish or yellowish and fire to buffs, creams or greys. Prepared stoneware bodies are based upon either ball clay or fireclay. Ball-clay stonewares are naturally plastic. Fireclay stonewares are plasticized. The difference is not immediately apparent in use but ball clays provide more strength and allow for a longer working period before tiring. Fireclay stonewares are acceptable for swift throwing, pressing and slabbing.

Porcelain is made from specially prepared bodies composed of plasticized china clay, feldspar for slow vitrification and silica for hardness and glassiness. True porcelain has a translucency which gives it depth even when too thick to allow light to pass completely through it. Semi-porcelain owns this quality in much lesser degree and is more correctly a white stoneware. Some white earthenware bodies make excellent semi-porcelains fired to 1200° to 1240°C (2192° to 2264°F) and are marketed as such. Bone china and translucent non-bone china are too short to use in plastic state but are available as prepared casting slips.

Clay for salt glazing

In salt glazing, volatilized salt combines with alumina and silica to produce the glaze. The best clays for salt glazing are fireclays which are high in silica. These have alumina: silica ratios of 1:5 and higher. Extra silica is sometimes added to clays as quartz sand but silica in isolation does not take a glaze.

Naturally occurring clays

There are many fireclays which have always been used for making saggars, cranks (kiln furniture) and wads (rolls of clay used to seal saggars). The important property of these clays is refractoriness and in the case of wad clay a refractoriness so decisive that virtually no vitrification takes place at all. These refractory clays have found expressive use in raku clays and as textural additions to stoneware bodies especially for architectural ceramics. Clays used in the production of firebricks and sewer pipes etc, often have dramatic possibilities for large scale slabbing, coiling and

Fig 43. Coarsely grained clay is used in this stoneware bowl by Frank Hamer. Thumb prints and partial glazing complement the texture of the clay. L. 14cm. (*Photo by Julian Sheppard.*)

modelling, giving rugged character to the clay statement.

China clay (kaolin) is the whitest burning of the clays. Because it is almost pure kaolinite and contains few impurities it is highly refractory. Its refractoriness is often described as a cone number and its whiteness negatively by the iron content.

Ball clay is a highly plastic clay usually burning off-white to cream although some pinks do occur. The majority of ball clays vitrify in the range from 1200° to 1300°C (2192° to 2372°F). Ball clay is the basic ingredient of many stoneware bodies and is also added to cream-coloured earthenware to give plasticity and strength.

Process

Bodies are produced for specialized making by individual processes. For example the high plasticity and strength required for throwing is not requisite for jigger and jolley work. It is foolish

Fig 44. The strength of fired stoneware allows the use of a folded slice building technique in this starling by Janet Hamer. H. 14cm.

Fig 45. The smooth whiteness of the David Leach porcelain body enhances the darkened tracery of the modelling. Vase by Mary White. H. 17cm.

to imagine that a single clay can be suitable for every process. We therefore see references to throwing clays, pressing bodies, slabbing bodies and modelling clays. It should be noted that a modelling clay or body has properties of smoothness, strength and plasticity with a long range of workability during its drying. These are necessary in building a modelling on an armature. Such a clay may not fire successfully. Its primary use is modelling from which a plaster cast is taken.

Once-fire clays and bodies are those with no volatiles save water. They can be glazed in raw state and fired in combined biscuit/glaze firing. However most clays can be used in this way if sufficient precautions are taken.

Fig 46. (*Right*) A white feldspathic body containing 40% china clay grog is used in this semi-porcelain slabbed box by Frank Hamer. H. 10cm.

Fig 47. (*Above*) A small raku pot by Janet Hamer. The refractory clay is pinched out thinly to give an even section. H. 6cm.

Appendices

Appendix 1 Clay Suppliers

United Kingdom
The products of English China Clays Sales Co. Ltd., St. Austell, Cornwall, PL25 4DJ are supplied to small users through appointed distributors and clay blenders, and not direct to individual potters.
Small lot distributors are:

Anchor Chemical Co. Ltd., Clayton, Manchester, M11 4SR.
Fordamin (Sales) Co. Ltd., Free Wharf, Brighton Rd., Shoreham-by-Sea, Sussex.
Somerville Agencies Ltd., Meadowside St., Renfrew.
Whitfield & Son Ltd., 23 Albert St., Newcastle-under-Lyme, Staffs. ST5 1JP.

Suppliers of prepared bodies and raw clays are:
Fulham Pottery, 210 New Kings Rd., London, SW6 4NY.
Harrison Mayer Ltd., Meir, Stoke-on-Trent, Staffs. ST3 7PX.
Moira Pottery Co. Ltd., Moira, Burton-on-Trent, Staffs. DE12 6DF.
Podmore & Sons Ltd., Shelton, Stoke-on-Trent, Staffs. ST1 4PQ.
Potclays Ltd., Brickkiln Lane, Etruria, Stoke-on-Trent, Staffs. ST4 7BP
Thomas E. Gray & Co. Ltd., 37 Headlands, Kettering, Northants.
Watts Blake Bearne & Co. Ltd., Park House, Courtenay Park, Newton Abbot, Devon. TQ12 4PS.
Wengers Ltd., Etruria, Stoke-on-Trent, Staffs. ST4 7BQ.

United States of America
Hammill & Gillespie Inc., P.O. Box 104, Livingston, NJ 07039.
Anhowe Ceramic Supply Inc., 4810 Pan American Freeway NE, Albuquerque, New Mexico 87109.

Cedar Heights Clay Co., 50 Portsmouth Rd., Oak Hill, Ohio
45656.
Firehouse Ceramics, 238 Mulberry St., New York City, New
York 10012.
Imacco Clays, Industrial Minerals Co., 1057 Commercial St.,
San Carlos, California 94070.
Kentucky—Tennessee Clay Co., P.O. Box 67, Mt. Union Sta.,
Alliance, Ohio 44601.
Minnesota Clay, 8001 Grand Ave., So., Bloomington, Minn. 55420.

Other addresses
Geological Survey maps of Great Britain are obtainable through
all Ordnance Survey agents, booksellers and map stockists
throughout the U.K. Maps required by educational establish-
ments may be ordered direct from Ordnance Survey, P.O. Box 32,
Romsey Road, Maybush, Southampton S09 4DH.

Sieves for the screening of clay are obtainable from most
suppliers of prepared bodies. Special sieves which can be nested
one above the other for test sieving of material to obtain residue
at different mesh sizes are obtainable from Endecotts Ltd.,
Lombard Road, Morden Factory Estate, London SW19 3UP.

Appendix 2 Analyses of Popular Clays

(kindly provided by the producers and suppliers)

	SiO_2	TiO_2	Al_2O_3	Fe_2O_3	MgO	CaO	Na_2O	K_2O	loss
English China Clays									
Standard Porcelain China Clay									
	47.2	0.05	37.4	0.6	0.2	0.2	0.1	1.7	12.3
Grolleg China Clay									
	47.7	0.03	37.2	0.7	0.25	0.1	0.1	1.95	12.06
Hymod TLD Ball Clay									
	55.0	1.3	30.0	1.3	0.5	0.3	0.5	3.2	8.7
Hymod SMD Ball Clay									
	65.0	1.4	23.0	1.0	0.4	0.2	0.4	2.4	6.8

ultimate analysis

	SiO$_2$	TiO$_2$	Al$_2$O$_3$	Fe$_2$O$_3$	MgO	CaO	Na$_2$O	K$_2$O		loss
ultimate analysis										
Moira Pottery Stoneware Clay	59.7	1.6	25.55	1.44						9.46
Podmore & Sons David Leach Porcelain Body	61.4	0.06	26.35	0.58	0.33	0.31	0.77	3.8		7.03
Watts Blake Bearne										
CC China Clay	46.8	0.1	37.4	0.8	0.2	0.1	0.1	1.7		12.8
HVA/R Ball Clay	62.7	1.5	24.8	0.9	0.3	0.2	0.3	2.3		7.1
TWVA Ball Clay	50.5	1.0	32.8	1.0	0.3	0.2	0.3	2.2		11.7
BBV Ball Clay	71.3	1.5	18.8	0.8	0.3	0.2	0.3	1.9		4.9
Cedar Heights									P$_2$O$_5$	loss
Redart Clay	64.27	1.06	16.41	7.04	1.55	0.23	0.4	4.07	0.17	4.78
Goldart Clay	57.32	1.96	28.5	1.23	0.22	0.08	1.18 (Na$_2$O + K$_2$O)			9.39
Firehouse Ceramics Hammill & Gillespie Blackbird (Barnard) Clay	59.7	0.67	10.87	14.65	0.75	0.27	0.12	2.04	MnO 3.4	7.48
Industrial Mineral Products Albany Slip Clay	57.64	0.4	14.66	5.2	2.68	5.78	0.8	3.25		9.46
Kentucky—Tennessee										
Old Mine 4 Ball Clay	53.8	1.7	30.0	0.9	0.3	0.3	0.3	1.1		11.8
Tennessee 5 Ball Clay	53.8	1.4	28.9	0.9	0.3	0.2	0.5	1.6		12.4
XX Sagger Ball Clay	56.7	1.7	29.2	0.7	0.3	0.5	0.3	0.9		9.9
Minnesota Clay										fired analysis
Plastic Vitrox (PV)	76.16		12.38			0.48	3.23	7.72		
Jordan Stoneware	67.2	1.18	20.2	1.73	0.52	0.16	0.23	2.0		6.7
Potclays Oxidising St. Thomas' Body	67.7	0.84	20.05	1.91	0.36	0.43	0.31	1.42		7.01
Reducing St. Thomas' Body	69.72	0.87	18.83	2.01	0.33	0.83	0.55	0.58	Mn$_3$O$_4$ 0.01	5.27
Pyropot Toasted Body	56.63	1.42	31.76	3.46	0.74	0.59	2.26	1.78		6.04
Special Stoneware	61.8	0.65	26.3	1.02	0.31	0.65	0.44	1.31		7.62
Smooth Stoneware	57.0	0.82	25.0	3.9	0.58	0.55	0.25	1.8	Mn$_3$O$_4$	9.8
Red S/E Body	58.0	1.5	24.0	11.0	1.0	1.6	0.2	1.5	0.2	fired analysis

	proximate analysis			particle size analysis microns						percentage retained by mesh	
	kaolinite	*micas*	*quartz*	<0·5	1	2	5	10	20		
English China Clays											
Standard Porcelain China Clay						70		95		0·03%	300's
Grolleg China Clay						57		90		0·05%	300's
Hymod TLD Ball Clay	54	34	10	50	75		96			0·5%	300's
Hymod SMD Ball Clay	41	26	31	41	57		75			3·0%	300's
Watts Blake Bearne											
CC China Clay	79	15	3	18	28	43	73	94	99	0·03%	300's
HVA/R Ball Clay	40	23	33	42	56	67	82	89	96	0·6%	120's
TWVA Ball Clay	61	23	12	54	67	78	90	96	98	1·2%	120's
BBV Ball Clay	28	20	49	28	37	46	65	79	94	1·0%	120's
Kentucky—Tennessee											
Old Mine 4 Ball Clay				62							
Tennessee 5 Ball Clay				41							
XX Sagger Ball Clay				43							

Appendix 3

This chart is an example of the sort of information which should be sought during sampling.

Stage 1

Name This is usually a personal name which serves as a reminder like 'yellow deposit at the bottom of the slope'.

Sample Is it typical or hand-picked? Would larger amounts be the same or does the deposit vary noticeably?

Description Colour and general description. First reactions to its feel are useful, whether sticky or spongy, gritty or smooth. On-the-spot tests: pinching a small pot, simple deformation test, tie-a-knot test, bite test, palm test.

Processing of sample Details may be important here for example whether the sample was dried and slaked or blunged as dug; and whether tap water or rain water was used. Mesh size of sieve or sieves should be noted and commentary made on its de-watering nature, whether uniform, sudden or partial.

Stage 2 Working properties

Workability These are the important comments upon the clay's usefulness for a particular purpose. Comparison with a known clay helps accuracy and later understanding. Include colour, texture and strength.

Leatherhard Comment upon strength, burnishing properties and fitting of slips, whether rewetting by slips causes distortion and blistering.

Dry Comment upon strength. Note any tendency to effervesce which could cause unsightly marks on unglazed work.

Stage 3 Fired properties

Initial tests will be small amounts fired on scrap pieces of kiln shelf. From the hottest and coolest parts of the kiln information can be built up about the firing range of the clay. More specific tests will be tiles and pots etc. with reference to the desired end product.

Firing range To establish the firing range note the temperatures at which the clay achieves sufficient fired strength, becomes dense, bloats, deforms and melts. Some clays have a wide useful range but others are restricted to exact firing conditions. Strength can be judged by comparison with other known clays.

Shrinkage Comparison with other clays is made by using percentage linear shrinkages. A convenient method is to make a small tile and mark a 10 cm distance on it. This is re-measured at dry and fired stages. Ten centimetres which is 100 mm provides an ideal initial measurement because percentage shrinkages from the plastic state are immediately available by subtracting the measurement in millimetres from 100.

Porosity Comparison with other clays is made by using percentage absorption figures. A sample piece of fired body is weighed, then placed in boiling water for one minute and left in the water overnight as it cools. The sample is wiped dry with a damp sponge and reweighed. From these measurements the percentage absorption is calculated thus:

$$\frac{\text{weight of saturated sample minus original weight}}{\text{original weight of sample}} \times 100$$

Unglazed appearance Colour, colour variation and surface texture.

Effect with known glazes Glazed colour. Whether the clay increases or inhibits fusion, causes pinholing or gives discolouration and whether the glazes fit without crazing or shivering.

Appendix 4 Recipes for Casting Slips

(kindly provided by clay suppliers)

	weight of dry clay	water	soda ash	sodium silicate 140° TW
Cedar Heights Redart Clay 1800°—2000° F	663g	337cc	1.4g	6.4g
Harrison Mayer Bone China Body 1240°—1250° C	1000g	450cc	—	3.3g
Harrison Mayer Stoneware Clay 1180°—1250° C	1000g	400cc	—	4.7g
Kentucky—Tennessee 1900°—2200° F OM 4 Ball Clay	16 lbs			
Tenn 5 Ball Clay	16 lbs			
Whiting	4 lbs			
New York State Talc	64 lbs	45 lbs	1 oz	6 to 12 oz
Barium Carbonate	up to 1 oz			
Moira Stoneware Clay 1200°—1240° C	1½ cwts	2½ galls	3½ oz	2¾ oz
Podmore & Sons David Leach Porcelain 1200°—1280° C	5000g	2960cc	—	9.9cc
Podmore & Sons Red Terracotta Clay 1100°—1160° C	5000g	1900cc	13.9g	30.7cc(75° TW)
Podmore & Sons White Earthenware Body 1100°—1160° C	5000g	2000cc	7.1g	5.5cc

Appendix 5 Recipes for Special Bodies

Wengers Egyptian Paste. (Recipe supplied by Wengers Ltd)

Soda Feldspar	40
Flint	18
China Clay No 1	15
Ball Clay No 4	5
Sodium Carbonate	12
Whiting	5
Fine Silver Sand No 1	8
Bentonite	2

Colourings:		
	Copper Oxide	1—3
	Manganese Dioxide	2—3
	Cobalt Oxide	1—2
	Chromium Oxide	1—2

First grind together dry ingredients then add only sufficient water to make a stiff paste. During drying the soda crystallizes on the surface where it develops a glaze upon firing to 980°C (1796°F).

David Leach Translucent Porcelain Body (Recipe supplied by David Leach)

Grolleg China Clay	53
Potash Feldspar	25
Fine-ground Quartz	17
Quest White Bentonite	5

This body is throwable and is normally fired to 1280°C (2336°F) in reduction. This body was marketed by Podmore & Sons Ltd. David Leach is at present researching an improved composition which will also be marketed by Podmore's.

Harrison Mayer Bone China Body (Recipe supplied by Harrison Mayer Ltd)

Calcined Bone	49
Cornish Stone	25
China Clay	25
Ball Clay	1

This body is for casting and jolleying. Firing temperature 1240°C (2264°F).

Appendix 6

Simplified origin of clays

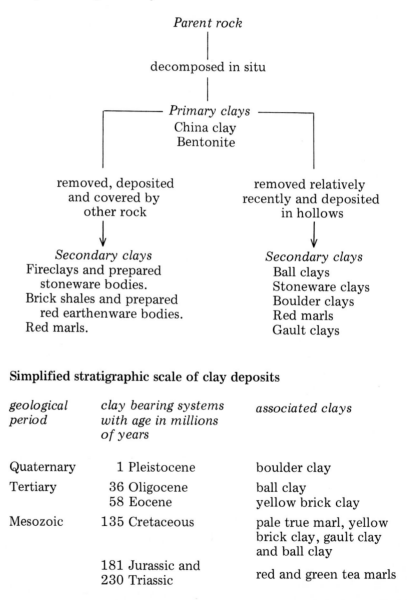

Simplified stratigraphic scale of clay deposits

geological period	clay bearing systems with age in millions of years	associated clays
Quaternary	1 Pleistocene	boulder clay
Tertiary	36 Oligocene	ball clay
	58 Eocene	yellow brick clay
Mesozoic	135 Cretaceous	pale true marl, yellow brick clay, gault clay and ball clay
	181 Jurassic and 230 Triassic	red and green tea marls

geological period	clay bearing systems with age in millions of years	associated clays
Palaeozoic	280 Permian — probable period of china clay granite intrusions	
	310 Carboniferous	red marl, fireclay, stoneware clay and brick shale
	405 Devonian	red marl
	425 Silurian	yellow and grey shale

Appendix 7 Measurements

weight equivalents

1 tonne	= 1000 kg
1 kg	= 1000 g

gross or long measure (UK)

1 ton	= 20 cwt
	= 2240 lb
1 cwt	= 112 lb
1 lb	= 16 oz

net or short measure (US)

1 ton	= 20 cwt
	= 2000 lb
1 cwt	= 100 lb
1 kg	= 2·2046 lb
1 g	= 0·0353 oz
1 gross cwt	= 50·803 kg
1 net cwt	= 45·359 kg
1 lb	= 453·6 g
	= 0·4536 kg
1 oz	= 28·35 g

length equivalents

1 metre	= 100 centimetres
1 centimetre	= 10 millimetres
1 yard	= 3 feet
	= 36 inches
1 foot	= 12 inches
1 metre	= 1·0936 yards
	= 3·2808 feet
	= 39·3696 inches
1 centimetre	= 0·3937 inches
1 yard	= 0·9144 metre
1 foot	= 30·48 centimetres
1 inch	= 2·54 centimetres

pint weight equivalents

oz pt UK	oz pt US	SG	°TW
26	21·7	1·30	60
26·4	22	1·32	64
27	22·5	1·35	70
27·6	23	1·38	76
28	23·3	1·40	80
28·8	24	1·44	88
29	24·2	1·45	90
30	25	1·50	100
31	25·8	1·55	110
31·2	26	1·56	112
32	26·7	1·60	120
32·4	27	1·62	124
33	27·5	1·65	130
33·6	28	1·68	136
34	28·3	1·70	140
34·8	29	1·74	148
35	29·2	1·75	150
36	30	1·80	160

Appendix 8 Bibliography on Clays and other Raw Materials

EEC Ball Clays Ltd: *To make one vessel unto honour.* (English China Clays, St. Austell, Cornwall, 1974)

H. Bennett and W. G. Hawley: *Methods of Silicate Analysis.* (Academic Press, London, 1964)

M. Cardew: *Pioneer Pottery.* (Longman, Harlow, Essex 1969; St. Martin's Press, New York, 1971)

A. E. Dodd: *Dictionary of Ceramics.* (Littlefield, New Jersey, 1964; George Newnes, London, 1967)

R. W. Ford: *Drying.* (Maclaren & Sons, London, 1967)

R. W. Grimshaw: *The Chemistry & Physics of Clays and Allied Ceramic Materials.* (Ernest Benn, Tonbridge, Kent, 1971)

F. Hamer: *The Potter's Dictionary of Materials and Techniques.* (Pitman, London, 1975; Watson-Guptill, New York, 1975)

G. W. Himus and G. S. Sweeting: *The Elements of Field Geology.* (University Tutorial Press, Cambridge, 1965)

W. G. Lawrence: *Ceramic Science for the Potter.* (Chilton, Philadelphia, 1972)

B. Leach: *A Potter's Book.* (Faber & Faber, London, 1949; Transatlantic, New York, 1973)

F. Moore: *Rheology of Ceramic Systems.* (Maclaren & Sons, London, 1965)

D. Rhodes: *Clay and Glazes for the Potter.* (Chilton, Philadelphia, 1959; Pitman, London, 1962)

L. & C., Rolt: *The Potters' Field — A History of the South Devon Ball Clay Industry.* (David & Charles, Newton Abbot, Devon, 1975)

W. Ryan: *Properties of Ceramic Raw Materials.* (Pergamon, Oxford, 1968)

A. B. Searle: *British Clays, Shales and Sands.* (Charles Griffin, High Wycombe, Buckinghamshire, 1912)

A. B. Searle: *The Clayworker's Handbook.* (Charles Griffin,

High Wycombe, Buckinghamshire, 1953)

A. B. Searle: *Refractories for Furnaces.* (Crosby Lockwood & Sons, London, 1948)

F. Singer and S. S. Singer: *Industrial Ceramics.* (Halsted Press, New York, 1963; Chapman & Hall, London, 1971)

W. E. Worrall: *Clays, their nature, origin and general properties.* (Maclaren & Sons, London; Transatlantic, New York, 1968)

W. E. Worrall: *Raw Materials* (Maclaren & Sons, London, 1964)

Various Authors: *Handbooks on Regional Geology of Great Britain.* (HMSO)

These books are now out of print.

Glossary

Adsorption The action whereby water is attracted to and concentrated on dry clay particles.

Agate-ware A decorative ware made from partially blended dark and light clays which give striations in imitation of agate. Slips are sometimes marbled with similar effect.

Albany clay An alluvial deposit on the Hudson River used for making slip-glazes.

Alluvial Material deposited by a river.

Ball Clay A highly plastic near-white fine clay. In the 18th and 19th centuries it was dug and transported from Devon to Stoke in football-sized balls.

Boss (of rock) An uplifted rounded dome typical of granite formations.

Biscuit To fire ware unglazed in preparation for glazing; also the unglazed fired ware.

Black-hard clay The stage of drying between leatherhard and white-hard. The clay looks its darkest with whitish edges.

Blunging Thoroughly mixing materials and water in a tank with centrally rotating impellor blades.

Body (1) The clay part of a pot which when fired can no longer be called clay.

(2) A prepared clay for a special purpose.

Bone-ash Ground calcined bones. A source of calcium phosphate used as a flux in bone china bodies.

Bone-china White, translucent porcelain with a lower temperature glaze. Ox bone-ash is used to flux the body to imitate the character of Chinese porcelain.

Bone-dry clay The last stage before clay begins to be changed to pot. All the pore water has been dispelled.

Boulder clay A clay of glacial origin containing boulders. It is a fusible clay suitable for soft-fired earthenware.

Brick clay A natural clay suitable for architectural ceramics but too coarse and short for potting.

Card-house structure Positioning of mutually attracted particles so that they build an open pore structure.

Card-stack structure The alignment of clay particles so that they can be closely packed as in compressed clay or a deflocculated suspension.

Chamotte Artistic wares made from coarsely grogged clay, from the French word for grog.

Cheese-hard clay Clay dried to the consistency of hard cheese.

China Clay Kaolin. The purest, natural white clay essential for porcelain and bone china.

Collodial size 0·3 to 0·001 microns. Smaller than the wavelengths of visible light.

Country (of rock) Older rock into which newer matter has intruded.

Crank mixture Fireclay or other refractory clay for making kiln supports. It is also used in raku bodies and coarse stoneware.

Crystal A geometrical formation of solidified mineral. Each mineral dictates a specific shape.

Culm clay A variable fireclay found with coal measures and gritstones.

Deflocculation A method of dispersing the fine clay particles in a suspension so that it becomes more fluid.

De-watering Drying. Reducing the water content.

Dipping The immersion of clay items in slip or biscuited items in glaze slop to give them a uniform coating.

Dunting Cracking of pottery caused by stresses which occur during firing and cooling.

Earthenware Any pottery body which, when fired, has a porosity of more than five per cent. This usually means ware fired below 1100°C (2012°F).

Elutriation The separation of fine clay from coarser clay in suspension by setting the whole in motion and allowing the finer particles to float away.

Encaustic tiles Tiles in which the pattern is inlaid with clays of a colour different from that of the body.

Engobe Slip. Buffer layer. A coating between body and glaze applied to improve texture or colour. Usually but not necessarily a clay slip.

Fat clay Fine, highly plastic clay.

Fettling Trimming excess clay or smoothing at leatherhard or dry stage.

Filter-pressing Dewatering slip to plastic clay. The press forces the slip through pervious bags where it solidifies into cakes.

Fireclay Coarse refractory clay found in association with coal measures and used originally for firebricks.

Flocculation The alteration of the electrostatic charges of fine particles in a suspension so that they are mutually attracted into flocs.

Flux An oxide which promotes ceramic fusion by interaction with other oxides.

Fusion The melting of different materials into an homogeneous liquid mass.

Gault clay A true marl of the Upper Cretaceous System of sedimentary rocks. It contains a high percentage of calcium carbonate.

Greenware Raw ware. Completed clay shapes not yet dry enough for firing.

Grog Ground fired body added to clays.

Hard-paste 'Grand-feu'. Vitrified, white, translucent porcelain in which both body and glaze are fired to $1300°C$ ($2372°F$), and over.

Igneous (of rock) Originating from magma. Cooled volcanic matter.

Jigger-jolley Forming clay shapes on spinning moulds by operating a template on the outside (jigger) or the inside (jolley).

Kaolin China clay. $Al_2O_3.2SiO_2.2H_2O$. The purest clay approximating closely the idealized clay mineral.

Kaolinite $Al_2O_3.2SiO_2.2H_2O$. Hydrated aluminium silicate. The idealized clay mineral composed of hexagonal flat crystals.

Kneading Preparing clay by hand using a rolling and spreading action.

Lawn Sieve. A fine wire mesh for separating particles in suspension.

Lean clay Short clay.

Leatherhard clay An unspecific term for clay ware that has dried to a state suitable for handling and turning.

Levigation The process of passing a thin slurry through a series of traps where the heavier particles settle and finer particles overflow.

Long clay Clay with high plasticity and strength, excellent for throwing.

Luting Joining together two pieces of clay in leatherhard condition by scoring the area and wetting with slip or water.

Magma A mass of molten rock.

Marl True marl. Malm: A natural earthenware clay containing iron oxide and calcium compounds. Known also according to source as Delft, Keuper, Tea, Kimmeridge, Gault and Weald marls. Some other iron clays without the calcium content are less correctly called marls, e.g. Etruria marl.

Maturing (1) Clays which are stored damp mature or improve in quality by the processes of ageing and souring.

(2) Each clay has a maturing range during firing in which it becomes progressively more compact and glassy.

Metamorphic (of rock) Changed by heat.

Micron One millionth of a metre.

Mineral A natural material which has a definable molecular structure and a distinct crystal formation.

Mould (1) A form made of plaster or biscuit with a negative shape on which clay is given shape by pressing, jiggering, jolleying or slip casting.

(2) Organic growth on stored clay which indicates that souring is taking place.

Ochre Iron oxide ores and ferruginous clays. Used to give brown and red colours or yellow when associated with lime.

Open clay Coarse clay or clay mixed with coarse grog or sand to give it an open texture.

Opener A material added to a clay to improve its workability to assist drying or discourage warpage. e.g. grog, sand, fireclay, sawdust.

Oxide A chemical combination of oxygen with another element.

Parian paste A soft-paste porcelain used for unglazed figures.

Paste A prepared 'clay' for a special ware, usually of the porcellaneous type. A paste contains below forty per cent of clay content.

pH value The measure of the acidity of a solution. A pH below seven indicates acidity, above seven indicates alkalinity.

Pipe clay Pure clays, marls or fireclays containing little or no iron from which tobacco pipes were made.

Pitchers Grog made from the same clay as that to which it is to be added.

Plastic clay (1) Clay ready for use.

(2) A fine slippery clay.

Pressing Press moulding. Forming pots by pressing plastic slabs onto and into absorbent plaster moulds.

Primary clay Residual clay. Clay found in its place of origin, most commonly, china clay and bentonite.

Pugging Mixing and compressing clay by putting it through a pug-mill.

Raku A Japanese word for 'enjoyment' now used for the process whereby red-hot glazed pots are withdrawn from a special kiln and reduced individually.

Refractory Resistant to high temperatures. Also an object made from such material.

Rich clay Fat clay. Fine, highly plastic clay.

Riddle A coarse mesh for separating the largest particles from crushed dry clays and shales.

Sand Natural ground quartz. Pure silica sand is used for frits and glazes and for placing. Less pure sands are used to open or speckle clay bodies.

Screen A sieve or riddle used for separating by size the grains of material either in suspension or dry mixtures.

Scumming Light-coloured marks appearing along edges and as finger prints on unglazed ware and biscuit. Caused by soluble salts in the clay which crystallize at the surface as the water evaporates.

Secondary clay Sedimentary clay. A clay which has been removed from its place of origin by natural forces and deposited elsewhere.

Sgraffito Scratched decoration especially when the scratched line or area scores through slip to reveal another colour.

Shale Clay which has been highly compressed under rocks into flaky pieces or soft stones.

Short clay Lean clay. Clay which has little plasticity and strength.

Slip A homogeneous mixture of clay and water used to coat clay forms to give colour and good surface.

Slip glaze A glaze that contains over fifty per cent of clay and is applied as a slip to the raw ware.

Slurry An uneven mixture of clay or glaze and water which is too lumpy to be called a slip.

Sodium carbonate Soda ash. Na_2CO_3. Being highly soluble it is fritted with feldspar and used widely as a flux in glazes. Also used as a deflocculant.

Sodium Silicate Water-glass. Na_2SiO_3. A combination of soda and silica soluble in water and used as a deflocculant.

Soft paste 'Petit-feu'. A white translucent porcelain in which body and glaze mature together at a lower temperature than hard-paste usually below 1200°C (2192°F).

Stoneware A hard, strong and vitrified ware, usually fired above 1200°C (2192°F), in which the body and glaze mature at the same time and form an integrated body-glaze layer.

Terracotta Earthenware modelling both glazed and unglazed. The word comes from the Italian and means simply fired earth though it is often used to describe the orange-brown colour of the red burning clay.

Thixotropy The property of slips at rest to become more viscous and of soft clay to hold its shape.

Tight clay A potter's term for fine, dense, de-aired clay which seems to have too much resistance for hand-shaping and is prone to cracking.

Tired clay Clay that has lost its strength by being over-worked.

Treading clay Kneading clay using the pressure of the bare human heel.

Underclay A softer fireclay from under coal seams sometimes mined with the coal.

Vitrification The furthest point to which a clay body can be fired satisfactorily. It is then dense, non-porous and partly glassy.

Wad clay Extremely refractory and friable clay used to seal saggars and support shelves in kilns.

Warping Twisting out of shape caused by unequal making stresses, uneven drying, or over-firing.

Water smoking Pre-heating. The drying of clay during the early stages of firing.

Weathering The natural breaking down of clay material promoted by sun, rain and frost.

Wedging Mixing and compressing clay by hand.

White-hard clay Nearly bone-dry clay. Almost any colour of clay will become white on thin edges.

Index